a little bit of
reiki

a little bit of
reiki

an introduction to
energy medicine

VALERIE OULA

STERLING ETHOS
New York

STERLING ETHOS
New York

STERLING ETHOS and the distinctive Sterling Ethos logo are
registered trademarks of Sterling Publishing Co., Inc.

Text © 2019 Valerie Oula

ISBN 978-1-4549-5895-6
ISBN 978-1-4549-3369-4 (e-book)

For information about custom editions, special sales, and premium
purchases, please contact specialsales@unionsquareandco.com.

Printed in India

2 4 6 8 10 9 7 5 3 1

unionsquareandco.com

Cover design by Kaylie Pendleton
Interior design by Erik Jacobsen

Cover images: Shutterstock.com: Dolka (hands); Muhammad Mahrus (lotus)

Interior images: Getty Images: DigitalVision Vectors/Pobytov (5, 98); Courtesy of
Wikimedia Commons (25, 64); Shutterstock.com: Dolka (hands); Muhammad
Mahrus (lotus); bc21 (28, 29); MrVander (33); Bejavisa Ruangvaree (66);
aninata (84); marinini (109)

contents

INTRODUCTION vi

1 • VIBRATIONAL UNIVERSE 1

2 • WHAT IS REIKI? 9

3 • REIKI ORIGIN AND HISTORY 23

4 • WHY REIKI? 31

5 • TYPES OF REIKI 37

6 • DIFFERENT LEVELS OF REIKI 51

7 • GET STARTED WITH A REIKI SESSION 59

8 • MOMENTS OF HEALING 69

9 • HOW TO MEDITATE 83

10 • HOW TO DEVELOP SPIRITUALITY 95

11 • THE ILLUSION OF GOOD AND BAD ENERGY 105

ACKNOWLEDGMENTS 109

ENDNOTES 110

BIBLIOGRAPHY 112

INDEX 113

ABOUT THE AUTHOR 116

INTRODUCTION

"And above all, watch with glittering eyes the whole world around you because the greatest secrets are always hidden in the most unlikely places. Those who don't believe in magic will never find it."
—ROALD DAHL

The Reiki system is a healing modality that opens you to the world of vibrational energy, the world of practical magic, the magic of possibilities. Reiki widens the human lens to receive more light, to see with more clarity, to take in a wider perspective.

Back in the day, I was one of those people who would roll my eyes at the mention of drum circles and shamans. My lips would curl into a slight sneer at the mere mention of angels and spirit guides. Yet, on the flip side, I followed astrology and definitely had at least one childhood encounter with a ghost, as well as spot-on readings from two psychics that tested the boundaries of my understanding. Being a born and bred New Yorker means that I'm a natural-born skeptic. However, I'm also open enough to give something a try at least once or twice. And once I've had an experience for myself and know it to be true, I want to shout it from the rooftops.

Whether you are well versed in alternative healing modalities or are just beginning to get curious about there being more than what meets the eye, whether you are a skeptic or a believer in things of a seemingly magical nature, or if you are a full-on spiritual seeker, there is one thing that is true and science based that we can all agree on:

Everything is energy.

And it is upon this foundation that we build—it's a mutual agreement and common ground on which we can all expand our shared knowledge.

The term *reiki* has probably been floating around your consciousness for some time, or you may have heard of it but never actually experienced it. Or, perhaps you got a massage and they did a little bit of Reiki but you never quite understood what it was. In whatever way Reiki has floated into your consciousness, you are finally ready now to learn a bit more about it. And here you are. There are no coincidences, ever—that is what Reiki teaches. We are living in a vibrational, holistic, connected world.

REIKI FINDS YOU WHEN THE TIME IS RIGHT

Reiki was my spiritual gateway drug. Once I experienced Reiki, I fell down the rabbit hole of energy medicine and spirituality. I had no spiritual or meditation practice when I first encountered Reiki. Working in beauty and fashion in New York City in my twenties, I was all about partying and going out, looking good and going to the "in" places; I was only concerned with outward appearances while my inner landscape was fraught with anxiety and just a plain old mess.

As I got older, my partying ways began to dissipate, but my inner landscape still had not been properly tended to.

It wasn't until I received a brochure in the mail from a local spa listing Reiki as one of its services that I decided I had heard about it enough times that I should finally go experience it for myself. When I arrived for the session, the practitioner didn't prepare me, and since this was before the age of Google, I had no idea what was going to happen. So as I was lying there, I peeked my eyes open for a quick second to find her holding a pendulum over me. Even though my eyes were closed, I managed to roll them hard. I could not believe that I had ended up in this place with some New Age whack job dangling a chain with a piece of crystal attached over my head and calling it a spa treatment.

Though my body was tense, I tried to relax and eventually the chatter and judgment in my head subsided and I drifted into a space of relaxed awareness. By the end of the session, I had seen swirling colors and felt like I was flying through space, seeing the galaxy and soaring through it. After the session, the practitioner told me that she sensed a giant gaping black hole in my solar plexus, which I guess sounded pretty bad, so she then tried to make things better by also telling me she saw blue butterflies around another part of my body. At this point, she might as well have told me about angels because that's the kind of hard, cynical city kid I was—butterflies and angels were the stuff of sappy greeting cards and I had no tolerance for any of it.

She wasn't the right practitioner for me at the time, but I definitely got what I needed, whether I knew it or not. It was easy for me to dismiss the relaxation I had experienced during the session, since I was really tired, and I explained away the soaring through space part by chalking it up to fertile imagination. My first Reiki experience was relaxing, and that's about it—or so I thought at the time. At the end of that year, during my first-ever meditation experience, which happened in a small Buddhist temple in New York City, I saw swirling blue colors and clearly heard that I needed to learn Reiki. Since I'd never "heard" anything like that before, I took it seriously, and signed up for Reiki training the very next day.

With Reiki, as with everything else in life, it's never time until it's actually time.

Just a note that we will refer to "Reiki" here as the Japanese term for life-force energy, and when capitalized, to mean the "Reiki system," the modality as taught by Master Usui. And now with this book in hand, it is time to explore the vibrational world that we are a part of. Let's just begin with a little exercise.

Take a moment here.

As you read these words, take a long deep breath in and slowly exhale out. Take a moment here to settle into your body, shoulders relaxed; feel your body relaxing into your seat, sinking into the support, and take a few more deep breaths in and out.

As you continue reading, slow your breath down and begin to soften any places of tension in your body. Visualize sending your breath into those places of tension, breathing in and out. Follow the breath in and out. Gently notice the space between the in breath and the out breath. Gently notice the pause between the out breath and the in breath. Allow each breath in and each breath out to create space in your body and in your mind. Allow yourself to open to receive whatever it is you need in this moment.

When we take time to pause and simply tune in to our breath, we bring ourselves into the present moment.

When we pause to observe our breath and tap into the space between breaths, we take ourselves out of ordinary time and space.

Suspension of disbelief is necessary when we play or when we want to be entertained. I've seen it when my cat hunts her toy mouse, which she knows is not real. We do this every time we read a novel or immerse ourselves in the experience of a movie. We are all capable of taking a moment to suspend disbelief, no matter how skeptical we are or how extraordinary things may seem. When we open our minds and our hearts, we can let go of thinking that we already know everything via what we can see and touch on this material plane.

I am inviting you to read this book, and as you go through it, to set aside what you think you know and to let the energy of the words flow through you, in whatever way feels right for you. Simply reading these words and ideas and stories may begin to open up new possibilities in your brain, in your cells, and in your very being. And when we open to possibilities, our lives begin to change.

In the most basic terms, the Reiki system is a hands-on healing modality. One reason for Reiki's popularity is that it's super simple to learn and it seems as if almost everyone knows someone who practices Reiki. Today, in the Age of Aquarius, there's been a major shift in acceptance of alternative practices and what was considered "New Age." Looks like we are fully in the New Age now that meditation has found its way to boardrooms, crystals are sold everywhere, and yoga is as common as running on a treadmill. Reiki is so popular now that it almost feels like it is a prerequisite for any healing practitioner's training. Through this book, you will get a taste of what Reiki is about, maybe just enough to whet your appetite.

1

vibrational universe

"If you want to find the secrets of the universe, think in terms
of energy, frequency and vibration."
—Nikola Tesla

Everything is energy. Even though matter seems solid, when we break it down to its smallest molecular particle, everything is vibrating. Every particle is vibrating at a certain frequency. When something vibrates at a slower frequency, it appears more dense. When something vibrates at a higher frequency, it's lighter, less dense.

Many people go about their daily lives thinking that things only exist on the gross physical level of what they can see, hear, taste, smell, and touch. There are those of us who only believe in the cold hard facts. So, here's something even the most scientific minds can agree on: the majority of what exists in the universe is unknown—how's that for a cold hard fact?

Familiar with the terms *dark matter* and *dark energy*? These are scientific terms we use to describe properties that scientists can't figure out, even though they know that they make up most of our universe.

The fact is that what we "know" in terms of actual matter only accounts for about 4 percent of what makes up our universe; the rest of that 96 percent is unknown and unseen. Let's remind ourselves of that fact when we come across ideas of energy healing that seem a bit "out there." Allow yourself to open to a richer world filled with magic and possibility—the idea of the unknown already exists in a scientific context, after all.

Isn't it awesome when the cold hard facts begin to chip away at what we thought we knew for sure, that essentially there is so much more than meets the eye?

As the science begins to catch up with the vibrational world, finding different ways to explore, capture, and measure that which is unseen, we find much of what ancient wisdom has shared with us through yogic knowledge, Traditional Chinese Medicine and studies like Kabbalah, and other types of mysticism actually correlates with new scientific findings. Some of it is being proved true now only because we are finally able to create what's needed to measure and show what might have been considered nonsense at one point in time.

Is it true that the Abominable Snowman and the Loch Ness Monster don't exist? Or is it just that we haven't quite figured out how to track and measure and "find" them?

For instance, from concepts such as ancestral karma to the tree of life, our technology is advancing so that we can begin to catch up with what ancient wisdom has been referencing on its own terms. There's the Large Hadron Collider in Bern, Switzerland, which is the most powerful machine created to date. Its purpose? To test particle physics and other unsolved questions, as well as to find other dimensions. Yes, other dimensions! Scientists are working to prove that there are many more dimensions than the one we collectively experience, which is somewhat mind-blowing whether you're a skeptic or not!

In the ancient Jewish mysticism of Kabbalah, there is the tree of life and its ten curtains that separate what is seen and unseen. The science that matches this concept can be found in physics' superstring theory, which states that there are ten dimensions versus the standard three and the fourth dimension of time.

And then there's the concept of ancestral karma, which is now actually proven through the study of epigenetics: trauma and depression in families can actually be passed down through the outer sheath of DNA. If those patterns of trauma and depression can replay themselves through generations of families, why not limiting beliefs and patterns of self-sabotage? Thankfully, it's not all bad—the good news is that resilience may also be passed down through families as well.

All of these are small examples of ancient wisdom meeting science. It's so fascinating when modern science finally catches up with age-old concepts.

Quantum physics shows us that we are living in a vibrational universe. We are surrounded by energy. We *are* energy. In the space that surrounds us, in the air around us, are billions and billions of particles of energy like radio waves, ultraviolet waves, microwaves—the list goes on. What may seem like empty space is actually teeming with activity, and when we intentionally tap into that space, we can cause an effect.

According to Lorenz's Chaos Theory and the butterfly effect, the minuscule flapping of a butterfly's wings in one part of the world has the potential to create huge weather systems in another. Everything is connected. Every action has a subsequent reaction, especially on a quantum level.

Mind blown yet? And if not mind blown, do you at least feel more questions bubbling up than answers? Getting curious about what you thought you knew about the world? Nothing is as it seems in this multidimensional, vibrational universe.

In the context of the vibrational universe and fractal cosmology—the self-repeating patterns that are found throughout nature—comes the ancient wisdom: "As above, so below. As within, so without." We are the macrocosm in the microcosm. In the yogic lineage, it is said that the energy of the planet is contained in our fingertips, and when we tap into this energy through specific hand positions called *mudras*, we can balance out our bodies, our universe. We can balance out the elements of nature through our bodies as well, since we are water, fire, earth, air, and ether. When we affect the structure of our bodies, we can change our lives, according to Dr. Randolph Stone, the founder of polarity therapy. Polarity therapy is an alternative healing modality. It is the study of the human energy field, and its practitioners work through and around the body to bring balance into the field.

As Dr. Bruce Lipton, author of *The Biology of Belief*, writes, "Humans are a fractal image of society, cells are a fractal image of the human. In fact, cells are a fractal image of society as well. The fractal nature of evolution is further implied by the reiterated, self-same patterns observed in each of the three cycles of evolution."

Our solar system consists of a sun with planets orbiting around it. Our planet Earth contains the moon and other quasi-satellites orbiting around it. Atoms contain a neutron with protons and electrons swirling around it. Our cells contain a nucleus with other organelles surrounding it. Fractal cosmology shows us patterns that repeat themselves on the macro and micro level. The pattern of branching is seen in a tree trunk through its branches and again in the natural waterways of our planet. Rivers branch out into tributaries. On the micro level, a human's lungs also bear this image of a trunk and its branches.

Everything is intertwined. We are all connected. We are fully immersed and a part of this universal energy, creating waves in a giant sea of energy throughout our known and unknown universe and multiverse.

Vibrational energy medicine? Yes, it's really a thing because of all the reasons mentioned. This is the idea behind why holding crystals affects change. This is why chanting mantras affects change. This is why sound healing meditations are all the rage. This is also the main reason behind why energy-healing modalities like Reiki work.

VIBRATIONAL UNIVERSE EXERCISE

You can read this aloud and record it on your phone and then play it back for a full guided meditation experience.

Let's take a guided meditative journey. Sit comfortably in a chair, with your feet uncrossed and grounded. Take a deep breath in and exhale. Close your eyes. Slow your breath down. Go within and move through your senses. Take a few moments to tune in to your body. Feel the support throughout your body, settling into your seat, allowing your body to be fully supported. Just begin to pay attention in a neutral way, inside. Bring attention to your breath; feel how your breath moves in and out. Tune in to the physical sensation of breath moving in and out of your body. Tune in to your breath for as long as you like. Just observe your breath moving in and out. Take a few moments to listen.

Listen to all the sounds around you, without labeling or identifying them in any way. Take a few moments here to listen to all the sounds all at once. And now notice any sensation in your body, without labeling it in any way. Take a few moments here to simply observe the feeling of pure sensation. Now look through closed eyes and notice what you see through closed eyes, maybe seeing light or dark, colors or textures. Take a moment here and just watch.

And now bring your attention to the hair on your head. With your hair acting as your subtle energy antenna, tune in to your hair from the roots to the tips. Notice the air around your head and the top of your head, taking your time and feeling into that. Now tune in to your skin. Feel the air on your skin. Feel yourself breathing; imagine yourself breathing through your skin, slowly in and slowly out, breathing through the largest organ of your body, your skin.

Imagine breathing through every single cell in your body. We are multisensory energy beings. Take a moment now to tune in to all of this, your breath, your skin, what you are seeing through closed eyes, the sounds, the sensations, tuning in to the subtle vibration of the world in and around you. Now you are tuned in, charged up, and connected to your vibrational being in this vibrational universe.

what is reiki?

"Don't you know yet? It is your light that lights the worlds."
—Rumi

The word *reiki* comes from the Japanese kanji, "rei" meaning spirit/ universal and "ki" meaning life force. Pronounced "ray-key," Reiki refers to universal life-force energy. The system of Reiki healing uses the inherent natural universal energy within all of us to bring us into balance.

The Reiki system is a Japanese energy balancing technique for stress reduction and healing. Reiki helps alleviate many physical and emotional issues; it supports the body's natural balancing process. Reiki increases the relaxation response so that the body can reset. Reiki practitioners channel universal energy to help facilitate the body's innate healing process—allowing the recipient to heal herself emotionally and physically.

And yes, *channel* is "to be a channel." In this case, this means acting as a clear conduit for universal healing energy to flow through, from practitioner to recipient. And while we are at it, let's address the term *universal healing energy*, which basically means tapping in through our vibrational world to connect to what's needed to come into balance.

Reiki energy flows from the practitioner to the intended recipient: be it a person, animal, or plant, or a situation—Reiki does not discriminate. Because Reiki is a natural energy cleansing process, it is not always a simple and unilaterally positive experience. Sometimes Reiki brings things up to the surface. Worsening of symptoms may occur briefly, but that energy will clear and pass through you. Often, recipients will experience what is referred to as a healing crisis, simply meaning that things may get a lot worse as the clearing begins, so that whatever has been stuck and stagnant on the energetic level can be released and the body can come back into balance.

Reiki healing is subtle energy work, tapping in to the subtle energetic field. In Eastern medicine traditions, it is not just the specific illness that is treated. The person as a whole needs to be brought back into balance. It's a holistic approach—treating mind, body, and spirit. Today, Reiki is also used in conjunction with Western medicine and offered in many hospitals, as a complementary alternative healing modality. There have been many studies done on Reiki in hospitals where it's characterized as "biofield therapy" and has been shown to reduce stress and anxiety as well as speed up the healing process and greatly reduce pain.

I was part of a program at Mount Sinai Beth Israel Hospital in New York City that had funding to study the effects of the Reiki system and other alternative modalities, such as acupuncture and yoga, on pre- and post-operative patients. Whenever I worked with patients, we always started with checking in with their pain level, rating it from low to high on a scale of 1 to 10. Patients would inevitably fall asleep mid-Reiki session, and when they woke up, they were almost always more relaxed and their pain levels decreased or even went away completely. The study and program continued to get funding because the results were quite positive. When you are relaxed, your body can heal faster.

Energy is all around us. Everything is vibrating, according to quantum physics. When we allow ourselves to connect to Reiki/universal energy, we can tap into the universal flow. We tap into the oneness of all that is; there is no duality.

We are all connected with every thing and every being on this planet. When we intentionally focus and tune in to universal energy, we can reset and come back into balance by opening ourselves and becoming attuned to the frequency of the universe. It's this state of oneness that allows us to share and receive healing, ease, and balance.

*Dis*ease is simply an imbalance, being out of ease with the natural flow. Emotional and physical disturbances occur when we are disconnected from our true nature, forgetting our spiritual, divine being—our original state of wholeness, balance, and harmony.

Reiki is not religious. The simplicity of the Reiki system is such that one does not even have to believe in it to work: the Reiki energy still flows where it needs to go.

Reiki supports personal and spiritual growth. Reiki energy can be used to clear space and homes. It can be shared with food, water, plants, and animals. And the best thing is that it's so simple that anyone can learn and benefit from Reiki, even children. Reiki is gentle and noninvasive. It's suitable for everyone from pregnant women to babies, cancer patients going through chemo to those in hospice care. It's helpful for all stages of life and offers comfort in death.

The Reiki system uses a light, hands-on healing approach between practitioner and recipient.

The practice of Reiki for the practitioner involves self-care, self-treatment, and a nonreligious spiritual centering practice. A Reiki practitioner must be diligent in caring for himself first and foremost, in order to be a clear conduit for the universal energy to come through.

Reiki can be thought of as a system of spiritual healing. It is a valid, complementary support for Western medicine. *The Reiki system is not a replacement for conventional medical care and treatment, so please consult a licensed health-care professional when need be.* There is no "doing" Reiki. It's really about opening yourself to allow the Reiki to flow and go where it is needed. For practitioners, it's important to keep up the Reiki self-care in order to be in alignment and grounded in universal energy. The Reiki practitioner, through meditation and self-care treatments, becomes a clear channel for the Reiki to flow through. It is not the practitioner doing the healing. The only thing a practitioner needs to do is to become the clearest channel, getting out of the way so that the energy can flow through.

When we share Reiki with another, we are not "doing" the healing. There is no ego involved. We are creating an opening for the Reiki energy to flow, simply being conduits to facilitate the healing process for another and at the same time benefiting ourselves. There is no right way or wrong way to do Reiki as a practitioner, because there is no doing. There is simply opening and allowing and receiving Reiki.

BELIEF NOT REQUIRED

There is nothing religious about Reiki. Reiki still does what it needs to do, whatever the religion. It is essentially a spiritual system, but belief is not required. Reiki works for atheist, Catholic, Jew, and Muslim alike. Reiki works to bring whatever is needed whether you believe in energy healing or not. All that is required is an openness to receive it.

REIKI LEVELS AND ATTUNEMENTS

Here's a quick overview of what will be covered a little more in depth later: Reiki Level 1 is about self-care, receiving Reiki and learning how to share it with friends and family, and, most importantly, receiving it for yourself. Reiki Level 2 involves diving deeper into the system and learning symbols to transmit distance Reiki that transcends space and time. The first two levels are more of a personal practice for yourself and for friends and family. For a professional practice, more advanced training is suggested. Reiki Level 3 is considered the master level in which one can teach Reiki and share attunements. A Reiki attunement is what gives people the ability to share Reiki.

Attunements can be considered a spiritual blessing as well as a clearing process. It's the process and ritual of how one becomes a Reiki practitioner. It is through this process that the Reiki energy and lineage is passed down from teacher to student.

Reiki's popularity lies in its simplicity. It's simple and easy to learn and to practice. Your hands naturally go to different parts of your body when you have pain or discomfort. Everyone has the power of healing within their hands— getting attuned by a Reiki master teacher just clears that channel, making it wider, in a sense, so that you can draw in more healing energy for others and for yourself. A Reiki attunement is like a fast track to opening to universal healing energy, blasting through old emotional blocks of stagnant energy. The Reiki attunement opens up your channel. It allows you to tap in to healing energy.

Different schools of Reiki have slightly different ways of preparing and sharing the attunement process. Personally, I have my Reiki students prepare for the attunement process by refraining from alcohol, caffeine, and sugar, and preferably following a vegan diet, or at least a vegetarian diet, a few days before. I also ask that they pay attention to what they are absorbing through the news, conversation, movies, etc.—the effects of fear-based news and gossip are heavy on the nervous system. By making these preparations, the body is already clearing and already detoxing ahead of the attunement process. Mindfully preparing can make the attunement process more effective. It's like fast-tracking the fast track. However, the attunement process also works without this kind of preparatory work, because Reiki is potent like that. Again, different strokes for different folks, and by folks, I mean Reiki master teachers.

Speaking of different strokes, there are also many ways to learn Reiki. There are a few courses where you can learn Level 1, 2, and 3 all in one weekend and become an instant Reiki master. Or, you can learn in a more measured and practical way over the course of several weeks and/or months, years. You can learn Reiki in a class in person or online. What's most important is that you resonate with the person who's teaching the course. This is a vibrational world and as with anything, if you are drawn to a certain course or teacher, there's something there for you.

Let's start with the basics of what a Reiki session looks like.

A REIKI SESSION

Curious about what happens during a Reiki session? A typical private, professional Reiki session lasts an hour to an hour and a half. The recipient is fully clothed and lies down on a massage table. The Reiki practitioner will spend some time talking to the client about what he or she wants to work through, resolve, or balance. Throughout the session, the practitioner will either use a light touch, or her hands will hover over yet off the client's body. The practitioner will be intuitively directed to different areas of the body. Just because someone comes in with pain in a certain area of the body doesn't necessarily mean that is where the practitioner will be placing his hands. There are invisible energy lines running throughout our bodies connecting to different areas and organs—in the practice of Traditional Chinese Medicine, these energy lines are called meridians, and in the Indian yogic tradition, they are referred to as "nadis." So, for example, perhaps kidney issues might be worked through by placing hands on the feet, or vice versa. It's nonlinear thinking, because we are working with energy and a different set of constraints.

Recipients sometimes see colors or feel heat, and it's all just energy moving. Sometimes recipients drift off to sleep, allowing their conscious mind to get out of the way so that they can receive energy. And they aren't really sleeping, since they are usually aware of when the session has ended. They are most likely in an in-between state between awareness and light sleep. People are often a lot more relaxed after their session. After the session has ended, recipients are advised that even though the session is over, the energy is still working its way through the body. It's best to take it easy after a Reiki session: don't head to a party right after—some rest and quiet time is best. Recipients are advised to drink a lot of water to help the clearing and shifting energy work through. Many people report sleeping better after a Reiki session, or maybe they just find themselves feeling lighter and more organized in their bodies. The most important thing to remember is that people always get what they need from a session whether they realize it or not. It may not be what is expected, but it usually is what is needed, one way or the other.

How many sessions should you have? The number of sessions is something to be discussed between practitioner and recipient, and depends on the issue or imbalance being addressed. Since you and your practitioner will be working with subtle energy, several sessions will have a greater impact on your overall well-being. So, ideally, more frequent weekly or biweekly sessions are recommended initially, if at all possible. After that, you may want to transition into infrequent (but still important) touch-up sessions from time to time—but again, see what resonates for you. Keep in mind, this is energy medicine. Think about the time it took for the issue you're treating to show up in your body. It takes time to begin to unwind that energetic process.

If all this reading about Reiki has piqued your interest further, you might be interested in trying a Reiki session, or even just starting with a mini-session, through a Reiki circle. There are often local Reiki circles or meet-ups that a teacher organizes so that practitioners and nonpractitioners can share, practice, and experience Reiki—it's a way for new and seasoned practitioners to practice and for those who are curious to experience a little bit of Reiki. Reiki mini-sessions are sometimes offered at wellness pop-ups and events as well.

Or, maybe you are all ready to dive into a full Reiki session. That requires finding a practitioner, which will be covered in a later chapter. But, begin by thinking about who you might want as your Reiki practitioner. And how you might find such a person. Perhaps it's through word of mouth, or a friend of a friend knows someone and recommended her to you. Maybe you'll go online and find a website that speaks to you. It is important that when you go about finding a practitioner, you don't get too hung up on their level of certification—though, they should at least be at a Level 2 for a professional practice.

There is no official Reiki association board like the Yoga Alliance with its 200 hours required training for yoga teachers. There is nothing official about Reiki. There are a few self-styled Reiki associations, but no established number of hours for a minimum course of study. Teachers structure their program in any way they like, though there are set basics to teach in each level. So, because Reiki has no official structure, don't rely entirely on titles and levels. A practitioner can become a Reiki master in one weekend and have only been practicing for two weeks, while someone who's only reached Level 2 may have been consistently practicing for ten years.

Communicate with your potential Reiki practitioner. Ask how long they have been practicing. Even if it's just through email, you'll get a sense of them through their words. Check them out on social media. What comes through someone's social media feed is their aesthetic and their energy. See what vibes for you. Maybe you'll want to schedule a quick call with them to get a feel for their language and energy. Tune in to your intuition and see which practitioner your energy requires. The same applies to finding a Reiki teacher to learn from. Seeing who you resonate with is really the key—this is a vibrational modality, after all.

BEING AN EMPOWERED RECIPIENT

Always remember that as a recipient of Reiki or any other healing modality, you are always in control. Whatever a practitioner shares with you during or after a session, whatever messages they may receive or see for you—see if it actually resonates with you. Or take time and sit with what was shared with you to see if it actually rings true in your body. You will know what is true for you and what isn't. We have to remember not to give our power away to anyone, not even a healer, teachers, or even a doctor. Develop your intuition and listen to what feels right for you. Often, the best sessions are the ones where we don't overanalyze and just allow ourselves to be in the energy that is still integrating. Just trust that things are shifting without getting too much in your head about what things mean. The constant need to know and the constant search for answers especially when one is beleaguered often results in our giving our power away—to that desire for someone to tell us exactly what's wrong with us and how to make it right. The best practitioners share just enough to open possibilities in your system and give suggestions. Avoid the ones that definitively tell you what's wrong and what to do to fix it. Take everything you're given with a grain of salt, unless it truly resonates with you—and, if it does, then fully embrace it.

STRENGTHENING YOUR POWER EXERCISE

Find a quiet and comfortable place to sit in a chair where you can keep your spine straight and your feet on the ground or sit on the floor comfortably supported in a cross-legged meditative position. Close your eyes and take a few deeps breaths in and out. Long, slow, and deep. Settle into your body. Begin to visualize your energetic body, emanating from your physical body in whatever way feels right for you. With each breath in and each breath out, feel your entire body breathing: breathing through your skin, breathing through every single pore and cell of your being. Now, as you breathe through the physical body, feel that breath expanding your energetic body.

Rub your hands together in a circular motion, the palms rubbing together in a steady rhythm. Begin to feel the heat of the friction between your palms. Keep going here, and, after several minutes, pull your hands apart. Hold one hand about chest level with the palm facing down. Hold the other hand slightly below the navel with the palm facing up. Keep about 6 to 8 inches (15 to 20 cm) of space between the palms. Begin to imagine a golden ball of energy building between the palms. Build this golden ball of energy by switching hands in a circular manner, palms facing each other but still keeping that space between them.

Visualize and feel that golden ball of energy between the palms of the hands. Once you've built that energy up for several minutes, place one hand on top of the other, two to three finger widths below your belly button, which is your *dan tien*—the elixir field in the Chinese energy medicine lineage, the seat of your power. Take in that golden ball of light, strengthening your personal power. Take a few minutes here, breathing in this energy, and feel what it feels like in your energy center. Feel the pulsation through your hands. Feel the warmth through your body. Open to the potent healing power in the palms of your hands and strengthen your own power.

reiki origin and history

"The goal of life is to make your heartbeat match the beat of the universe, to match your nature with Nature."
—Joseph Campbell

There are so many myths and so much misinformation surrounding Reiki's history and the healing system's origins. You may have read that Reiki comes from Egypt or Tibet or even Atlantis, and that is simply not the case. The Reiki System of Natural Healing comes from Japan and was discovered and founded by a Japanese man named Mikao Usui in 1922. Master Usui was well traveled and had knowledge of many things, but what influenced him most was his Buddhist practice and the overall Shinto religion of Japan. Shintoism is an ancient religion in Japan. It recognizes that spirits live in nature.

It is the worship and respect of nature, from the sun to the trees to the water to the rocks. Shintoism also carries the ancient tradition of ancestor worship. Many in Japan practice Shintoism and Buddhism; they are complementary.

Mikao Usui was born in 1865 in the village of Taniai, Japan. He worked as a government official. He was well traveled and interested in different religions. He was married with children. In other words, he was a regular guy with no real superpowers, except that he was a spiritual seeker. He had a dedicated meditation practice and was also a lay Buddhist monk, meaning he had not denounced his worldly life, but would devote himself to the temple from time to time. Being a spiritual seeker, of course he was looking for more in life. In the 1920s, his teacher suggested that he take on a more severe retreat. He was advised to head up to Mount Kurama to fast and meditate.

Much of what we know about Master Usui is conveyed to us via the memorial stone inscription erected by his students near his gravestone. He headed up to Mount Kurama to search for inner peace and enlightenment. After fasting and meditating for twenty-one days, which left him feeling very weak, Master Usui felt as if he were struck by lightning through the top of his head, and passed out. When he awoke, he had the realization that all was one—that there was no separateness, no duality in this world. There is only oneness. He was so excited by this truth that he became filled with a great energy and started rushing down the mountain so that he could share this realization with everyone. As he was rushing to get down

MIKAO USUI   CHUJIRO HAYASHI   HAWAYO TAKATA

the mountain, he tripped and hurt his foot. As he hurt his foot, he automatically put his hands on the injury and he noticed that the pain immediately dissipated and his foot was healed. And from this moment, he realized that his hands contained healing energy: Reiki.

Mikao Usui began to see clients for healing work, and the news of his healing hands and presence spread around town. Soon he established a healing clinic and school in Toyko called Usui Reiki Ryoho Gakkai, and saw many clients. The foundation for his Reiki teaching is meditation. That was the key to connect to the oneness of the universe.

There are many miraculous stories of how Master Usui helped people through Reiki. The most famous story is probably the one from the time of the great earthquake of 1923 in Japan. In the aftermath of disaster and destruction, Master Usui helped many people who showed up at his clinic. At one point, there were so many people showing up hurt from the earthquake that he was sharing Reiki with several people at once—through his hands, his feet, his eyes, and his breath. Master Usui died from a stroke a few years later in 1926, after having taught two thousand students.

There are two more key figures in the development of Reiki. Chujiro Hayashi was a naval doctor who was a student of Master Usui's. Dr. Hayashi learned from Master Usui and brought his healing technique to the other naval officers. With permission from Master Usui, Dr. Hayashi codified his healing technique into a protocol and established levels of training, so that it would be easier to learn. Dr. Hayashi eventually opened his own Reiki clinic as well.

Let's just pause right here for a moment to appreciate the fact that an actual medical doctor in the early 1920s was so blown away by the healing techniques of Reiki that he opened his own clinic and trained other naval officers in Reiki. Many of the early Reiki practitioners were serious, disciplined naval officers doing hands-on healing.

The third figure in the story of Reiki is Hawayo Takata, who was an American woman of Japanese descent living in Hawaii. Madame Takata was quite ill when she traveled to Japan. She had gallstones, appendicitis, and a tumor. She was scheduled for surgery, but when she heard about Dr. Hayashi's clinic, she decided to go visit it. Once she had experienced Reiki, she put off the surgery to see if Reiki could help instead. She went on to receive daily treatments, and several months later, she no longer needed surgery.

Madame Takata was so impressed by the results that she wanted to learn Reiki herself. But at that time, Dr. Hayashi told her that it could only be taught to Japanese born in Japan. Madame Takata pleaded with him to teach her, and he finally agreed, but only if she committed to being at the clinic for a period of time for training and mentorship. And she agreed. She studied with Dr. Hayashi for a year. Once she completed her time in Japan, she traveled back to Hawaii and opened her own Reiki healing clinic in Hawaii with Dr. Hayashi's permission.

Madame Takata brought Reiki to the West in 1938. In order to make Reiki more palatable to an American audience, especially in the wake of the war, she fabricated stories about Master Usui, saying that he was actually Christian and had studied at the University of Chicago, which of course wasn't true. She spread the knowledge of the Reiki system throughout the United States. However, it wasn't until closer to the end of her life that Madame Takata attuned a handful of Reiki masters, twenty-two to be exact. She charged $10,000 per master level student. This wasn't out of greed, but rather out of wanting to make sure that this master level was revered and fully appreciated as sacred. By doing so, she also ensured the slow initial spread of Reiki teachers.

GROUND AND ELEVATE EXERCISE

This simple yet potent exercise comes from my teacher, Gary Strauss, cofounder of Life Energy Institute. It's a wonderful way to begin and end your day.

Connect to Earth

Take a comfortable stance with your feet slightly wider than your hips. Feel that grounding through your feet, through your legs. Imagine the earth under your feet, bend the knees slightly, and sweep your arms and hands out and down as if you are gathering and drawing up the earth energy. Pull up that earth energy with your hands, drawing up the midline of your body, and then push it up and out through the top of your head through the movement of your hands. Do this at least three to five times.

Connect to Heaven

Inhale, look up, and sweep your arms overhead, and then bring your hands to prayer position above your head, looking upward. Feel as if you are gathering in the infinite knowledge of the heavens. On the exhale, draw your prayer hands down through your head, your face, and the midline of your body as you draw down that energy of the heavens and the universe. Do this at least three to five times.

Connect Heaven to Earth

And then bring both movements together, first drawing up the earth energy and then drawing down the energy of the heavens. Do this at least three to five times.

At the end of the set, take a moment with a few deep breaths in and out to feel how energized you are, connected to heaven and earth.

why reiki?

"Energy cannot be created or destroyed, it can only
be changed from one form to another."
—ALBERT EINSTEIN

Reiki is about creating space in your life, in your mind, and in your body. Creating space opens up any stagnant, stuck energy in your system, in your physical body and home, in your energetic field, so that you can be in the flow of life. When we learn about Reiki, we can begin to remember that all is one and one is all. In the same way, Dr. Bruce Lipton's fractal evolution describes the cells in the body as mini-humans; we can make the parallel assumption that we humans are probably the cells of the earth, one holistic organism. And the beauty of the universe is that it is a self-correcting system: nothing is ever lost or gained—everything is contained and transformed and transmuted.

REIKI EFFECTS AND BENEFITS

Who might benefit from Reiki? Everyone. The beauty of Reiki is in its simplicity. Reiki's popularity has spread everywhere. And it's becoming so much more mainstream, which is why so many hospitals offer Reiki. Because of this, there are more and more studies done on Reiki every day.

Got an issue? There's a Reiki session for that. Reiki can help with issues such as anxiety, depression, insomnia, and fatigue, as well as physical aches and pains. Reiki may help people feel more balanced and give them a renewed sense of energy. More clarity and focus may also be an effect after a Reiki session. Ultimately, Reiki can bring more balance and flow into your life on a physical, emotional, and mental level. This healing modality grounds and restores your energy. It helps to bring energy into your system if you feel depleted, and it can ground excess energy as well. Regular Reiki sessions bring whatever energy you need to bring yourself and your life into balance. Reiki supports you through the process that is life. It helps you to open and trust the flow of the universe.

REIKI AND SYNCHRONICITY

When we begin to think about Reiki and universal life-force energy, we can tune in to the ebb and flow of life. Maybe you've

never considered it before, but when we start to pay attention in a different way, we can begin to notice how energy is all around us. We might even begin to notice synchronicity in life. You know that thing where you are thinking about someone and then they actually call you or you run into them—and you say, "You'll never believe it, but I was just thinking about you." Happens all the time. It's energy. *Synchronicity*—it's the term for meaningful coincidences described by psychologist Carl Jung. Life is filled with them.

Once you've experienced Reiki or learned and shared Reiki, or maybe just by reading about Reiki, you might just find that you notice more and more synchronicity in your life. As I write this book and have a minor freak-out about it not being good enough, in my state of mini-panic, I text a writer friend whom I haven't seen in many months to ask for advice. And, of course, he responds back that he was just on his way to my meditation class, which means we can talk later. Synchronicity in action.

Early on in my journey of self-development, I decided to ask the universe for a sign of life. I think I might have whispered something like, "Okay, universe, if you are listening, please show me a sign: show me a red ball today"—which was a totally random request. I made this request early in the morning, and by end of day, I had completely forgotten about it. On the subway going home, I saw a poster from a public art illustration series by Sophie Blackall. It's a simple illustration of people sitting on a subway train. It depicts subway riders and their belongings on a commute, along with a red ball that is shown bouncing from one end to the other through the subway car. And when I noticed the red ball that I asked for, I smiled to myself, because the ball is depicted twice. But that smile turned into a full-on laugh when I noticed that the illustration of the people on the subway car has a mini-version of the same illustration in the illustrated subway car—basically an illustration within an illustration that shows another red ball . . . and following the logic of this illustration within an illustration, this goes to infinity, as does the red ball. I asked for a red ball. The universe showed me a red ball to infinity. It's kind of crazy, right? The universe does not play small. It is a full-on baller status. (Baller is slang for a ballplayer who lives an extravagant lifestyle.) The universe takes my one measly red ball and delivers unto infinity.

Once you've opened up to Reiki or even the idea of Reiki, you may find more and more synchronicity in your life. There are no such things as coincidences; those coincidences are instances of you cocreating with the universe.

TUNING IN EXERCISE

Are there instances of synchronicity in your life that come to mind? Take time to begin to tune in to the energy of the universe. The universe is always communicating with us, if we only pause to listen. Take some time to notice any signs or recurring elements that you notice through the day or the week. Make note of these recurring images or phrases.

See if what you are noticing speaks to you in terms of a message or a wake-up call. Don't make yourself crazy that everything is something. Use this as a tool to wake up and be more conscious. Don't spend your time analyzing every little sign—that's not living your life, nor being in the flow. Just take the time to observe and notice without being too hyperfocused. If you are deliberately seeking and looking, you won't find it. Take a relaxed approach, be chill, and just observe, without attachment to outcome. This is just an exercise to tune in to paying attention. Universal life force energy, *reiki*, is all around us. If we can stop long enough to listen intently, we can develop our spiritual connection with the oneness of the world. We are always being nudged and given signs through synchronicity. Learn to listen to the universe and you'll be rewarded richly.

5

types of reiki

"The beauty of the universe consists not only of unity in variety, but also of variety in unity."
—UMBERTO ECO, *THE NAME OF THE ROSE*

As with anything that is simple and true, many different variations can branch out from Reiki as we understand it. As you read more about Reiki, it may be that you'd like to explore this modality for yourself. Doing a search for a practitioner will bring up a myriad of options as well as various types of Reiki. There are now many different types of Reiki, each branded to its particular teacher, with its own different spin.

When Madame Takata initiated her twenty-two Reiki masters in the United States, it was through an oral tradition, so she never gave handouts, and her students all had their own separate notes. As many of her students started working with the Reiki energy, some began to add additional symbols and attunements, effectively creating new variations of Reiki. Many of her students started to channel additional symbols and tap in to different ways of bringing other healing practices and terms into the Japanese system of the Reiki they had learned. Many of these different types of Reiki work with various concepts such as angel guides, chakras, auras, and crystals—which are definitely more Western and not at all Japanese.

There's the original Usui Reiki Ryoho, which is what was taught by Dr. Hayashi and simplified further by Madame Takata. My suggestion is to always go with what speaks to you. There isn't one type of Reiki that is better than the other; it's just a matter of preference and resonance. Go with what resonates for you when you read through or research more.

Here are just a handful from over a thousand types of Reiki:

Jikiden Reiki and Komyo Reiki are fully Japanese traditions that claim to follow Master Usui's teachings most closely. Gendai Reiki Ho is a modern mix of Japanese and Western Reiki traditions.

Raku Kei Reiki requires a Reiki master level certification before receiving the additional attunement and symbols. This modality was created by a student of Madame Takata, Iris Ishikuro, and brought to the West by her student, Arthur Robertson. Raku Kei is said to be Tibetan in nature and incorporates chakras, mudras, breath work, and additional symbols.

There are several types of Reiki created by William Lee Rand: Usui/Tibetan Reiki combines traditional Reiki with elements of Raku Kei Reiki. Karuna Reiki adds additional symbols and attunements after the traditional master level has been achieved, and is said by its practitioners to be more potent than the original Reiki system. The newest, Holy Fire Reiki, claims to be even more refined and comes from a higher level of consciousness.

In addition to the types of Reiki created by William Lee Rand, there is Seichem, an ancient Egyptian healing art similar to Reiki, channeled by Patrick Zeigler in 1980. Kathleen Milner brings Seichem and Reiki together along with additional symbols to create the Tera Mai system.

Radiance Technique is termed "Authentic Reiki" and "Real Reiki" by Dr. Barbara Ray, who says that this is the only authentic Reiki as originally taught. Radiance Technique has seven levels of attunements and "secret" keys given directly and solely to her by her teacher, Madame Takata.

And in this Age of Aquarius, it seems as if there are new styles of Reiki popping up all the time: Shamanic Reiki, which combines Reiki and shamanic practice; Crystal Reiki, combining Reiki with the use of crystals; and Kundalini Reiki—all are examples of Reiki systems that have proliferated in the recent past. I used to be a real stickler about keeping Reiki pure and original, as it was taught. Over time and with experience as a teacher and a student of different modalities and traditions, I've learned that it's best to start with a solid foundation—to know the original teachings as a foundation and master it. And once you've mastered the basics, only then can you begin to improvise and add on. When I teach Reiki, I teach it as it was taught to me—using the Usui method. In my actual practice and sessions with clients, I use a more integrative approach. These days, I let clients know that what I practice is not straight-up Reiki. And, trust me, I was a by-the-book practitioner of classical Reiki protocol for many, many years until it was time for me to open up and recognize that all the modalities that I've learned can come together in one session. We live in a new day and age. People evolve and teachings evolve.

Reiki as originally taught by Master Usui is a very simple system—its foundation is to cultivate a deep spiritual practice. Cultivating a spiritual practice begins with meditation. It is only through meditation and getting quiet that we can begin to know ourselves and listen to our own inner wisdom and cultivate compassion for ourselves and others. Through consistent meditation, we can begin to get clear and to discover who we truly are. In Master Usui's system of Reiki, it is meditation and the attunements that help make the practitioner. The use of healing through the hands is almost a secondary aspect, a side benefit.

The term *reiki* was already in use when Master Usui began his system of Reiki. It's similar to the term Qi as in the Chinese energy work system, Qi Gong. The term refers to the universal life-force energy.

When we actually examine how Master Usui taught, his main teaching point was meditating upon the precepts. By learning to listen and connect to the universe through meditation, we can heal ourselves and draw down that universal energy to help others as well. Master Usui's original teaching did not include symbols or hand protocols—this all came about because Dr. Hayashi had asked Master Usui for more to help him teach his naval officers. So symbols were given and a step-by-step hand protocol was introduced.

To sum up the Usui method of Reiki, it's all about meditation and attunement. Receiving attunements helps to clear and open up awareness. Usui's teachings recommend that students keep meditating in order to open up awareness even more. Master Usui received Reiki through meditation, so it makes sense that this would be his main approach to sharing Reiki. In order to practice and share Reiki, you must help yourself first through self-care. Kind of like when flight attendants remind you to pull down the oxygen mask and secure it for yourself to breathe before helping someone else in case of an emergency.

WHICH REIKI?

As you can see just from these few examples, there are a whole lot of Reiki choices out there. And everyone claims their technique is the purest, highest, best Reiki out there—and what if that's true? Maybe it is true that each and every Reiki technique is the "best," because there are so many people resonating with different ways to connect and understand Reiki energy.

There is no right Reiki or best Reiki. There are teachers out there who are purists and feel that incorporating all these add-ons takes away from Reiki's simplicity, and that may be true, too; however, people vibe with what they vibe with. I may certainly still roll my eyes at websites that claim that Buddha came down to them and told them to add more attunements to the Reiki system because it was incomplete, but that just means it's not for me personally but still could be for someone else. Find the thing that doesn't make you roll your eyes, and find the thing that actually feels right for you. You just have to find the one right teacher and find the Reiki that speaks to you and experience it for yourself.

PERMISSION TO RECEIVE

Permission and energy work is probably something that people don't think about much. Why can't people just go around sharing Reiki with others? If Reiki is gentle and self-regulating, it should be fine, right? Most people want to help others, so why can't they just share Reiki with anyone they like—doesn't that seem like a good thing? But that's not cool. You know when you are going through a rough patch and the last thing you want is someone smothering you with an unwanted hug? Their overconcern can be oppressive and stressful when you just want to be left alone. So yes, autonomy is key—as with all things, people have sovereignty and agency over their bodies and their energy fields.

This is a main sticking point for me when I teach Reiki to my students. Practitioners must always absolutely have permission from their recipients to share Reiki. It is a sign of respect, but also a huge reminder that we cannot force our will over others.

Those recipients from whom practitioners need permission might also include babies, animals, and people who are very ill and may be too incapacitated to directly respond. Even if clients can't use language, practitioners can still connect and ask permission through a meditative space and listen for the response. If the practitioner does not encounter or hear a definitive no, then they can proceed with the recipient's highest good in mind.

Ultimately, if the recipient is not open to receiving—no matter if they say yes or no—they will only take what they are open to.

My uncle had been ill for a very long time. He was in intensive care, and I had to wear a protective gown over my clothes so as not to transfer any germs to his already very weakened immune system. He wasn't able to speak, but we were able to communicate through writing and gestures. I asked him if he would be open to some Reiki and he nodded that that would be okay. As I placed my hands lightly on his body, it felt like the energy was bouncing back out, as if it were being repelled somehow. I am conscious of how I choose to interpret events, but it seemed as if the energy being drawn through my hands was then repelled. There was resistance. And when I realized this, I looked up at my uncle, who looked at me and shrugged his shoulders with an expression on his face that conveyed, "Nothing's happening, this Reiki stuff isn't working." He had always been a skeptic with a very logical engineer's mind. His face seemed to say, "This stuff is baloney, but I'm letting you try because you're my niece." With that, I knew that it wasn't the right time, and so I stopped. Even though he had given me permission, there was a part of him that was resistant. I do believe that what little bit of Reiki he was willing to accept—since it was being drawn through my hands—was what he needed and what he could process at that time. He did eventually make it out of the ICU, but he never recovered from his slow and debilitating illness.

Permission to share Reiki with another person or being who is willing to receive it is important. This doesn't apply to the short Reiki bursts that practitioners send to others as a blessing or as an extra boost of support. For instance, if someone is having a rough day or a big meeting, a practitioner sends a quick shot of energetic support, but for more sustained sessions, permission is absolutely necessary.

As a practitioner and teacher, it's important to remember to meet people where they are in life. We are only ready when we are ready. Respect everyone's path and their journey, no matter how much you think a modality or tool could help that person. Respect, compassion, and permission are key. That goes for all beings that we share Reiki with, including animals.

REIKI FOR ANIMALS

Reiki works through the biofield of any organic being, be it crystals, water, plants, human, or animals. Animals open to Reiki energy fairly easily, for the most part. Animals are also extremely sensitive to energy. When I first learned Reiki, I was so excited to share it with my cat, Booboo, that I forgot to ask whether or not she was interested. And when I lightly placed my hands on her, she got super annoyed and walked away. The next day, as I was recounting this story, my teacher said that as with any energy work, the most important thing you can do is to make sure that you have permission. Nowadays, the way I share Reiki with Booboo or any animal goes something like this: I let them know that I'm going to share Reiki with them and that they can take as much or as little as they need and they can end the session anytime they wish. This allows choice and free will.

Several years ago, I volunteered Reiki for an amazing nonprofit organization in New York City called Wild Bird Fund. They rehabilitate injured and sick birds and other urban critters, from pigeons, hawks, swans, and migratory birds to squirrels. There are so many stories of how Reiki has helped these little patients heal faster. There are also stories about how Reiki brings whatever is needed, whether or not the outcome is what we deem good.

There was a very sick seagull that the Wild Bird Fund asked me to work with, sitting in his cage. As I stood in front of the cage, I mentally let him know that I was going to share Reiki with him and he could take as little or as much as he needed for healing. Before we began, he was facing me, but when we started the session, he turned around and faced the other way, literally giving me his back. I could tell that he wasn't very interested in taking Reiki, but I sensed that he took a little bit anyway. I thanked him for taking what he needed. The following week, I returned. He was still there, but this time when I offered to share Reiki with him, he stayed facing me. It seemed as if he was nodding off, fighting sleep, but eventually he gave in and slept while the session continued, for about fifteen minutes. Then, when we were done, he drank a whole lot of water, which I have seen happen with animals after sessions. I thanked him for letting me share Reiki with him, and I was thrilled that he had opened up to the energy this time. When I returned the following week, I was really looking forward to working with him again, but sadly he had passed. He passed the day after our last Reiki session. It was as if during the initial session, he wasn't ready to face his death, but that little bit of Reiki helped him to open up. And after the following week's session, the Reiki energy helped him transition with ease.

There are so many interesting stories of animals and Reiki. Animals are the best ambassadors of Reiki's effectiveness—there's no talk of placebos with animals; their conditions shift one way or the other, they come into balance, and they get what is needed.

Whenever companion animals receive Reiki treatments, I always recommend that their guardians book a session for themselves as well. Our energy informs a large part of their energy. Our companion animal friends take on our stress and anxiety. They soak it all up, and so in the same way we need to regularly clear our energetic field, they do, too! For those of us who have companion animals that have developed chronic or debilitating illness, it's an opportunity to look within ourselves—not as a way of blaming ourselves, but as a way of getting curious about what emotional issue might be reflecting back.

When we first took in Theo, our little boy cat, rescued off the street at around six months old, he developed crystals, which blocked his ability to urinate. The vet recommended prescription food, but we opted to go the holistic route instead. *(This is a choice, knowing all the risks that we still choose to make for ourselves. This is anecdotal content. This is not intended as medical advice. Please consult your veterinarian regarding any health and medical advice for your companion animals.)* This consisted of more water, higher quality food, supplements, and Reiki, which helped him tremendously, and the condition resolved itself. But over time, he started developing constipation—it got so bad that he had to go to the animal hospital for a procedure for manual extraction. With knowledge and perspective, and under the treatment and care of our new holistic vet, I began to realize that our little boy cat was experiencing physical manifestations of stuck energy. This stuck energy reflected from the stuck energy of our apartment and relationship at the time.

When we are able to observe the energy within and around us, when we are able to see the patterns of energy, we can open ourselves to receive what we need to come into balance.

RECEIVE AND FLOW EXERCISE

Feel free to journal with these prompts:

- ❈ **Do you find it easier to give or to receive?**

- ❈ **Do you have a tendency to do more for others than for yourself?**

- ❈ **How open are you to receiving?**

- ❈ **Can you take a nice long, smooth deep breath in? Can you take a long exhale out?**

- ❈ **Are you able to receive gifts with ease?**

- ❈ **Are you able to ask for and receive help when you need it?**

- ❈ **What about compliments? Do you start hedging and downplaying the compliment and explaining why it's not true? Practice saying thank you even if you don't feel worthy of the compliment. It's a practice. And it allows you to open to receive.**

We work so hard to be self-sufficient and independent, which is great. But, as the poet John Donne reminds us and I paraphrase here: no man is an island unto himself. It's also important to be able to receive from others. It's important to give, but equally as important to receive. Burnout is a real thing in our society, with all its constant doing and even more doing in order to be productive. When we engage in that constant hustle to have to make things happen, we also need to remember to refuel and replenish and let others help us as well. When we take time to pause and just be, we can integrate and receive. We might also begin to notice that life flows when we flow and that flow begins with breath.

When you begin to track your breath, note the count of your inhale and the count of your exhale. Is one longer than the other? Is one more difficult and choppy? Notice the quality of your inhale and exhale. Practice breathing long and deep. Learn to slow down the inhale and slow down the exhale. See if you can slow down the inhale and the exhale in equal counts.

Our capacity to give and our ability to receive lies in our breath.

6

different levels
of reiki

"The Universe is under no obligation to make sense to you."
—Neil deGrasse Tyson

There are three levels of Reiki training. Each level includes attunements designed to open up the practitioner's system to receive more and more energy. The levels build upon each other, widening the practitioner's channel each and every time.

REIKI LEVEL 1

This level is all about self-care, which is the foundation of the Reiki practice. In this basic beginner's level, you'll learn about your own natural innate healing energy and how to tap in to it to care for yourself. A practitioner needs to take care of herself before helping another. The self-care practice is what keeps a practitioner clear and strong energetically. Without a strong foundational practice, the practitioner cannot be a clear channel for the healing energy.

Basic Level 1 training consists of attunements to initiate and open your ability to tune in to Reiki energy. During the attunement process, some may feel a tingling sensation or warmth in the hands, or feel emotions come up, or some may feel nauseated or have a headache. All of this is just energy moving and clearing, which is why a light diet cleanse may be recommended beforehand to clear your channels to connect you to the flow of Reiki. At this level, you'll also learn Reiki history, hand placements for self-care, and mini-session protocol to share with friends and family. This level is all about practice, practice, practice. Practice on yourself and practice on friends and family, even the skeptical ones. Explore and dive into this newfound energy that has always been in your hands!

REIKI LEVEL 2

In Level 2, we begin to delve deeper into the Reiki journey. We learn how to transcend space and time through Reiki. In this level, three healing symbols are taught, as well as a full body protocol of hand placements on how to share Reiki with a recipient lying down. Symbols are given so that we can get into the right frame of mind to work with our intentions. The symbols are an anchor and a focal point. We learn to draw and chant these symbols. Through the use of these symbols, we can heal the past and send support into the future. Reiki supports us through the process of life.

The Reiki symbols taught in this level help students get into the right state of mind for a session. The protocol gives the students a basic outline to work with until they reach the master level in which they are fluent with the language of the Reiki energy and have developed their own vocabulary of energy within. We also learn how to clear the energy of a room and how to do distance healing, which will be discussed later. Level 2 brings us fully into the energy of Reiki, and we can begin to experience it all around us. Here we are given Reiki tools which help us transcend space and time. There are some that may see clients after completing this level, though it is recommended to first complete Level 3 before doing so.

REIKI LEVEL 3

This is the master level. A fourth symbol is given in this level. And, essentially, at this level, we learn that there is no *doing* Reiki and that instead we are simply *being* Reiki. We are in the oneness of all that is, which allows us to open to the flow of life as it is. This master level is really a journey to know yourself. All the work we do at this level is to enable us to look deeply into our own inner landscape. To be a master is simply to delve into our own crap and clear it out, constantly, and to be fully aware and conscious of what we are projecting. Often, when it comes to levels of Reiki, we give these labels too much weight; regardless of the level, it is up to the individual to either coast along or truly do the work. Level 3 is technically the professional level, but, again, that can look very different depending on your own practice.

By the master level, the practitioners' intuition is much more developed and they have learned to trust and listen to that innate wisdom through their hands and their energy field. Beyond the master level, a practitioner becomes well versed in the language of energy and is discerning in what to share and in how to share it with students and clients.

It's important to reiterate that since self-care is the foundation from which any Reiki practitioner begins, don't hesitate to ask your practitioner if self-care and meditation is part of his daily routine. Again, tune in to your intuition and choose a practitioner that resonates with you, no matter what level.

DISTANCE HEALING

We mentioned distance healing as being taught under Level 2 training, but what is it, exactly? It's simply healing at a distance. Reiki healing can be shared long-distance. It might be hard to wrap your brain around that thought, but yes, indeed, distance healing is a thing. Quantum physics discusses the concept of nonlocality and what Einstein has termed "spooky action at a distance," and somewhere around these terms may be the key to how distance healing works. In a blog piece for *The Huffington Post*, Deepak Chopra explains:

"Quantum entanglement is another term for the principle we want to understand in this post, quantum nonlocality, by which tiny objects initially interact, then move any distance apart and still impact one another."

Maybe thinking about Reiki and its gentle hands-on healing approach is already a stretch, but we are going to stretch a little further and take it into distance healing. When I learned how to share distance healing in Reiki Level 2, it was just so amazing that I wanted to share it with everyone and anyone. I was so excited about distance healing that a complete stranger got to be a recipient, a guy who was working at the Genius Bar at the Apple Store. I had employed some Reiki symbols to help the long line at the Genius Bar move faster and was so psyched when the line flowed that I told my specialist all about it. He was intrigued, and I ended up offering him a distance healing session. Yes, I offered distance Reiki to a complete stranger because that's how absolutely excited I was about the phenomenon of distance healing.

Distance healing works as well as an in-person session. And if someone was nervous about trying a Reiki session, I would absolutely suggest starting with a distance session. One reason might be that when people are in the comfort of their own homes, they can relax and may be more open to receiving what they need. Sometimes a client lying on a massage table may feel a little vulnerable when a practitioner is working over his body. I would invite you to experience both: maybe begin with a distance session if you are a little nervous, and eventually book an in-person session.

WHAT HAPPENS DURING DISTANCE HEALING?

During a distance healing session, the practitioner and recipient both agree on a specific date and time. Distance sessions are generally about thirty minutes long, more or less, according to the practitioner. They need to agree on a mutual date and time for the session. The recipient shares with the practitioner what issue they would like Reiki to balance and support them with. Both practitioner and recipient set themselves up in a place where they won't be disturbed and where they can relax. You might set your space by lighting candles or using essential oils and crystals. The practitioner prepares the space to tap in to and transmit the healing energy. The recipient is seated or reclined in a comfortable space and open to receive. The practitioner shares the Reiki at a distance by employing Reiki symbols as well as through intention to connect to the recipient to help them with their healing request. Honestly, distance Reiki is just really cool. And now the scientific community is beginning to notice and starting the research.

Reiki can be used to support goals and groups as well as events in the future and in the past. We are living in a vibrational world, and we are all vibrational beings. So when we tune in to energy, we can transmit waves of healing the same way Wifi and Bluetooth connect our devices. Through the tools of distance healing, we can heal and balance our past so that we can step fearlessly into the future.

7

get started with a reiki session

*"At the center of your being you have the answer; you
know who you are and you know what you want."*
—Lao Tzu

When it comes to finding a practitioner for a Reiki session, do your
homework. And that homework is to find a practitioner who resonates with you. Check out their website. Google them. Ask questions. Communicate with your potential practitioner. How long have
they been practicing? Where do the sessions take place? Are there
pictures of the treatment room? Scour their social media. Get a feel
for the practitioner's aesthetic. Is it the right vibe for you? Nothing is
more off-putting than walking into a treatment space that's smoked
up with patchouli incense and filled with images and statues of

goddesses if that's not your thing. Aesthetics of the environment and practitioner can quickly set off your defense mechanisms, and if you want to get the most out of your Reiki sessions, you want to be as open as you can be. So do the prep work.

Often, practitioners work out of a rental space, and the decor reflects the owner of the space, so you can't always go by decor. Still, practitioners have a choice in terms of location, so while the decor may not be in their personal taste, they can work well in the space itself if it speaks to them. Make sure you pick a practitioner you like who is at ease in the location in which they are working.

Many of my clients have come to me through Instagram. Social media is energy. It's the energy that you put out there. It's an extension of the person behind the account, even if a lot of social media is highly curated and set up to paint a certain picture. It's still energy, and it's energy that reflects the often trite but also true saying, "Your vibe attracts your tribe." If what you see on a practitioner's social media resonates, they may be right for you.

Trust the combination of your research and your intuition. Take the time to truly consider your options. Engage with your potential practitioner via email or a phone conversation. Get a feel for their energy and see if they speak your vibrational language. Do so even if they were recommended by a friend. What works for your friend may not necessarily be your cup of tea. When you find the right person for you—you'll know!

HOW TO PREPARE FOR A REIKI SESSION

Once the practitioner has been decided upon and the session booked and paid for, something curious begins to happen. It may be subtle, but the Reiki energy begins to work on the recipient. There's energy in committing to the session. There's energy through the exchange of payment for the session. So get clear on what it is that you'd like to work through; while your problem may consist of several issues, it's best to focus on just a few things per session. It could be a physical or emotional issue or both, since one informs the other. It may be much-needed support to help achieve a goal or support to help break a habit or long-standing pattern. Think about what it is that you are ready to release and let go of, as well; let that be part of your intention for the session.

Make sure to bring or wear comfortable clothes to change into. Generally, professional sessions take place on a massage table where the recipient is always fully clothed. Some practitioners may burn candles or use sage or Palo Santo sticks to clear the space. Let your practitioner know if you are allergic to any essential oils or incense or sage beforehand.

DURING A REIKI SESSION

Always make sure that you are comfortable during the session, and if you are not at any time, be sure to let the practitioner know. If you are new to energy healing, feel free to ask questions as things come up, or you can save your questions for after the session. Before the session begins, the practitioner will discuss how the recipient would like to focus the session—what the intention is that the practitioner will hold for the recipient. Again, this is a reminder that it is not the practitioner doing the healing. It's the recipient's system that draws the Reiki energy down. Reiki energy is unlimited. There is no transfer of energy between practitioner and recipient, there is no exchange of personal energy—no one is taking on nor giving someone their personal energy. Reiki practitioners work with universal life-force energy and simply act as the channel. Reiki goes where it is needed.

The recipient may feel heat or feel areas of cold. She may see colors or visualizations. All of this is simply energy moving and shifting. The Reiki helps to open up any blocks in the system.

I like to think about those blocks in the system in this manner: as we go through our daily lives, little traumas and big traumas occur. Let's say someone angers you or hurts your feelings. In an ideal world, we would process those feelings right away. We would give ourselves time to identify what's happened and sit with our feelings and let them move through us. The reality is that painful feelings are uncomfortable, and we live in a society that values nonstop doing. So it's easy to tell ourselves that we don't have time to deal with the hurt. We energetically package up the hurt or the anger and we shove it off to the side—still somewhere in our energy field. At the end of the day, ideally, we would come home and say to ourselves, "Okay, now let's deal with that stuff that happened earlier." Locate those hurt feelings, and sit with them, feel them, and process them through your body and then let them go. Unfortunately, what usually happens is that we just don't deal with them at all. We are hardwired to avoid pain, so we brush it off and forget about it. Yet it is sitting there in a tight little package, in your energy field.

Over time, all those little instances of hurt and anger build up and start mucking up your energy field. And eventually all those emotional packets of stuck energy build and begin to have an effect on the physical body. People love to say things like, "It's so strange, everything was fine until I woke up one day and suddenly had this excruciating back pain." There is no such thing as "suddenly." It's been building up in the energy field, un-dealt with and unexamined. By the time you feel the pain, your body is trying to tell you something: that it's time to look at the stuff that you've been avoiding. Pain is your body's way of communicating to you that something is wrong and that you need to pay attention.

When we tune in to Reiki, not only do our aches and pains begin to shift, but our minds begin to shift as well. It may take a while, but it happens. Think of the effects of a Reiki session as slowly peeling off one thin layer at a time to get to our own true nature. Reiki works with the layers of subtle energy, so the work itself can be subtle. Of course, there are those who may have big shifts, monumental experiences, and profound healing in the very first session, but everyone is at a different place and space in their lives, and every subsequent session will also be different.

Oftentimes, as clients come regularly, the work becomes even more subtle. The first or second time may be more obvious in that initial clearing of energy, but as clients come regularly, the effects can be more nuanced. It's no longer the dramatic clearing but more like refinement. Reiki helps us to refine our energy, to clear and distill, to create space for our truth.

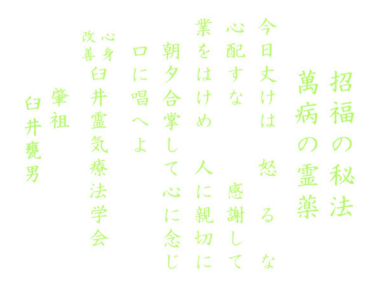

招福の秘法

萬病の霊薬

今日丈けは　怒るな

心配すな　感謝して

業をはけめ　人に親切に

朝夕合掌して心に念じ

口に唱へよ

心身改善　臼井霊気療法学会

肇祖　臼井甕男

CREATE SPACE

What are some ways you can begin to create space in your life?

How might you bring the principles of Reiki into your life to create space?

This is what Master Usui gave his students to meditate upon—the five Reiki precepts:

- Just for today, don't worry.

- Just for today, don't anger.

- Please accept everything and give thanks.

- Strive to embody the teachings in your actions.

- Be kind to yourself and others.

Take this time to reflect upon the Reiki precepts. Make it easy: just start with the first two. Bring them into your life to create space. When I first learned the precepts, I repeated the first one all the live-long day. In my previous career, I was a casting director and I produced photo shoots. One might say that I was well suited to producing shoots, because I was always thinking/worrying about things ten steps ahead of what was actually happening. I was the manager of the worry store, already anticipating ten fires and how to put them out if need be. It was so stressful, but also so much fun, and I loved it, all that rush of adrenaline . . . until, after several years, it was no longer fun and I was running on adrenal energy, which is akin to running on fumes versus actual fuel.

What was helpful to manage my stress early on was Reiki, and specifically the first precept: *Just for today, don't worry.* Don't worry, because nothing is actually under your control. Do your work as best you can and allow space for whatever happens to flow through. That is life: completely unpredictable. So, just for today and today only, don't worry.

We expend so much energy worrying about things that are out of our control. What a waste of energy! When people don't believe that thoughts are energy, invite them to consider how exhausted they feel when they are looping negative thoughts around in their head, worrying about things that most likely won't even happen, or even replaying some bitter drama or a situation in which they were wronged, over and over again in their minds. It's exhausting and a waste of time and energy. Be an efficient and productive energetic being. Take that energy and put it toward something that you'd like

to create instead. Use that energy in a positive and more efficient manner.

UNIVERSAL CONNECTION EXERCISE

Sit comfortably or lie down. Close your eyes. Place one hand on your heart and one hand either on your solar plexus or your belly; it doesn't matter which hand is where. Through this position, connect to the innate healing power of touch. Connect your heart with your power at the solar plexus or at the seat of your power by the navel. Just breathe long and deep here, breathing through those places of contact and coming into the energy of balance and healing. In the Reiki self-care protocol, this is called Universal Position. It is comforting and empowering at the same time—allowing us to connect to our heart space and our power. This is a nice way to start the day before you get out of bed, or end the day before you go to sleep.

8

moments of
healing

These are a few favorite Reiki moments from clients, students, and colleagues*:

A Reiki master practitioner, **Rachel**, shared this story about her husband, who is a super skeptic. He's very scientifically based and wasn't at all interested in trying Reiki. He eventually allowed her to share it with him and loved how relaxing it was. He now asks her to share Reiki all the time. She notices how supportive Reiki can be when it comes to her husband's immune system and how much less often he gets sick. Before Reiki, if he were to catch a cold, it would run for two miserable weeks. Now, when he feels a little run down with a cold coming on, she'll share Reiki and he'll only be sick for two or three days, which is a considerable improvement.

All names have been changed and all people have given permission to share their stories.

This same colleague was just recently home with her newborn baby. It was a day where she was completely overwhelmed—her little baby boy was crying incessantly and breast-feeding wasn't going well. She was in a lot of pain. She sat down with her baby lying on her chest and reminded herself to just breathe. Almost immediately, she could feel herself surrounded by Reiki energy—just flowing all around them, connecting her and her baby. And all became calm. It was magical, in her words.

Another colleague, **Deva**, used Reiki to help her niece prepare for grade school. She drove to school and infused her niece's chair with the Reiki symbol for grounding and focus. She drew Reiki symbols on the classroom door and lockers to bless the class. Her niece noted how well the first week of school went.

Deidre came to me with fibroids and wanted to see if Reiki could help so that she could avoid surgery. She was in her early thirties and going through some big transitions in her life. She had received Reiki several times before and found it very relaxing and helpful. During the session, I sensed the fibroids as tightly wound up, thick red strings of energy. As we continued the session, it felt as if they were beginning to unwind a bit, opening up a little. There was also a sense that this was related to not doing what she really wanted to do in life, that her creativity was stifled. And, in truth, she admitted that she was no longer sure what it was that she wanted, after being newly married and taking some time off to plan her wedding and build a house. She felt a bit lost and unsure of herself.

She continued to come for weekly sessions to work through the fibroids. It was discovered that most of the fibroids weren't that big except for one that seemed to be growing, and the doctors recommended surgery since she was hoping to become pregnant sometime soon. My client was extremely anguished about the whole process around finding the right person and place for her surgery. So the next few sessions were about balancing out the energy of anxiety as well as helping the fibroids. At our final session before surgery, I sensed that the fibroids were ready to be just scooped up and popped out. When the surgery finally came about, the very large fibroid, which was about the size of a grapefruit, came out so easily that even the surgeon was surprised. It was as if the fibroid was ready and primed for quick removal. My client felt that the Reiki sessions had helped to "loosen" and prepare the fibroids for what could have been a much more complicated surgery.

My cat used to get a leaky eye fairly often. Basically, one eye would get super watery and start to leak incessantly. Whenever that happened, the vet would prescribe an antibiotic ointment that I would have to put in her eye. It was always an ordeal to put the ointment on my finger and stick my finger in her eye—this is a feisty cat that we are talking about here, so the process was not fun for either of us. One day, I saw the start of leaky eye and realized that we were out of the antibiotics. I called my vet, who had to call in the prescription, and I was told I would be called when it was ready. In the meantime, wanting to help and not having medication, I shared Reiki several times throughout the day with my cat. By the time the prescription was ready, we no longer needed it. The leaky eye had come into balance. Another Reiki practioner, Donna, had a very similar situation with her cat, Kaia, as well.

A fellow Reiki master practitioner, **Annabelle**, was on vacation with a friend in Puerto Rico. Her friend was napping and somehow a curtain rod fell on her head. The friend was in some pain, so she offered a little Reiki to help. Quickly, Annabelle's hands shifted over to her friend's eyes—as she puts it, she was just following her intuition. Annabelle had forgotten that her friend was having eye difficulties: she was not forming tears, and had to go through a number of experimental procedures to create new tears from her platelets. Upon returning from vacation, the friend went back to visit her eye doctor, who checked her eyes. After months of issues, the doctor found absolutely nothing wrong. In fact, the doctor mentioned that had this been the first time ever seeing this patient, nothing would have been found to be wrong with her eyes.

A client in her late twenties, **Sara**, started coming to me with a list of issues that she wanted to work through. On the physical level, she had an involuntary facial twitch that she found annoying and problematic. She also had chronic sinus issues since she was young. After several sessions, the twitch lessened and the sinus issues got somewhat better. Sara came weekly to work through other issues as well.

Sara was a model client in that she was extremely self-aware and willing to see her own shortcomings. She was here to do the work and get results. The sinus issue felt like an ancestral issue. Her father had always had sinus issues as well. Even though the sinus problems got somewhat better with the sessions, she got to a point where she really wanted it taken care of completely and opted for sinus surgery back home over winter break. She had been told that it would be quick, with easy recovery and a good success rate. I like to remind clients that Reiki takes time; all energy work takes time, especially with chronic issues, but ultimately I'm here to support my clients with whatever they need to do for themselves.

When Sara returned from her break and we met for our session, she was so excited to share that she did not go through with the surgery after all. She decided to get a second opinion. The other doctor did an X-ray and found that Sara had an enormous amount of impacted old buildup in her sinus cavities. The first course of action was to loosen and dissolve the buildup and then perhaps revisit the idea of surgery at a later date if necessary. Sara was most excited to share this news with me because she remembered that in her first session, I had felt that there was a lot of old stuck energy in the places where the X-ray showed the buildup. We continue our work together to keep clearing.

Angela was in her mid-thirties and completely distraught over the breakup of her three-year marriage. She was depressed and inconsolable when she arrived for our session. She had been convinced that she and her husband were going to be together forever. She loved him and she loved the life they had together. It was a shock to her that he no longer wanted to be married. She was extremely sad and scared to be on her own. Her intention for the session was to find peace.

The session lasted an hour and, near the end, as I was working by her feet, I had an image of her dancing barefoot, joy-filled and carefree. She was wearing white and had flowers in her hair. She was dancing with a man who was spinning her off her feet. It looked like a wedding. I was reluctant to share this image with her since I thought it might upset her, but the feeling of joy was so strong that I had to. At the end of the session, she was much more relaxed. I shared the vision with her. She felt that it was her and her soon to be ex-husband because she saw a similar vision as well, but instead of feeling sad, she felt gratitude, thankful to have had the time together as a couple and having felt that joy and love. She was at peace.

Another colleague, **Cara**, shares a story about a friend who was scheduled surgery to address migraines and pain for years due to an issue with a compressed nerve. Cara and her friend discussed doing distance healing for three days in a row to support her recovery process. On the first night, when Cara started the distance session, she saw an image of her friend playing soccer. The friend was a big soccer player in high school and college. Cara felt a clear knowledge that her friend was going to be back to feeling better than ever quickly. It felt so reassuring, and Cara shared this feeling with her friend. The friend's recovery went smoothly. It was a comforting and profound experience for both practitioner and recipient.

Cara's own story was that Reiki brought her into her body. She was a big athlete growing up, but surprisingly it wasn't until she experienced Reiki that she realized how ungrounded and disconnected she was. Through Reiki, she finally had a solid sense of herself in a way that she had never known before. It was the first time that she was actually aware of her feet on the ground.

John was new to Reiki. He had just started meditating and found it extremely helpful for his anxiety. He was curious how Reiki might further help him. He arrived and shared that he was stressed about his work and finances. He had experienced surges of energy during meditation, but had never had an energy healing session before. As the session proceeded, he seemed to relax more. At the end as we wrapped up, his eyes popped open and he lifted his hands up and patted the table. He seemed a bit perturbed. He shared that he had the oddest sensation of floating up and feeling extremely light, so much so that he needed to make sure that he was still in contact with the massage table. Needless to say, he left the session feeling a whole lot lighter.

When **Kassandra** arrived for her first session, she was open to the experience but wasn't quite sure what to expect. Her intention for the session was to begin to heal the trauma of losing her father when she was a child. As the session started, almost immediately she could feel her body getting slightly hot and then slightly cold at certain times. Toward the end of the session, she felt like her hands had fallen asleep, but she could feel the electric energy shooting through her hands. She actually wondered if she was going to be able to use her hands again. Once the session ended, the energy began to subside and her hands went back to normal, but right then and there she knew that the energy she felt coursing through her body was real and that it had helped to unleash a lot of what she had been suppressing. That night and for two weeks afterward, she cried the most she had ever cried. It didn't matter where she was, the tears kept coming, and they didn't stop. I had mentioned in the session to her that whenever she was upset or wanted to cry, she needed to let it out. And she did just that. She felt that what was happening after that first session was allowing her to purge grief she had withheld for so many years. And in her words, it was an entirely new beginning for her and, even though she was crying, she had never felt better in her entire life.

Anne, in her early thirties, had a super successful branding company that she built from the ground up. She had created an amazing business and made a wonderful life for herself. The only thing missing was a meaningful partner. At the end of the day, she came home to a gorgeous but empty apartment. She was lonely. When we first started working together, her intention had been to stay spiritually connected and grounded. It was only through progressive sessions that we started uncovering and healing past trauma. Only once we started addressing the trauma was she able to realize that she was lonely. The intention of the sessions was never specifically to find a partner but instead to focus on her healing and her coming into balance. Several months later, after creating more space in her life to take care of herself first and foremost, she met someone whom she was able to build a loving relationship with.

Lisa, a Reiki Level 2 student, shares her touching story. She writes: "One of my early experiences with Reiki was one of the most rewarding and healing sessions I've ever received, so much so that it piqued my curiosity to study Reiki and embark on a wellness journey I couldn't have anticipated. I booked a treatment with my massage therapist who often incorporated bits of Reiki into our otherwise sports-therapy-related treatments. At the time of this particular session, I had lost my kitty of seventeen years a few days prior and knew I needed something more nurturing, so I requested a Reiki-focused session. I was in a very sad place and was emotionally drained after a couple of months of severe illness and the ultimate loss of my furry soul mate. I was blessed to be with her when she passed, but what I didn't realize prior to Reiki was that I was not really at peace with her passing.

"During my session, I became very relaxed and in a sleep-like state. All of sudden, I had this vision of a soft white and cloud-like light, and there stood my kitty, healthy and fluffy as ever, meowing at me as she did. I then felt my grandmother stand behind her. She was also a soul mate in this life and had passed sixteen years prior. When I felt her presence with my cat, I remembered the moment when I held my kitty as she was passing and I told her she would be okay and that my grandmother would be with her and watch over her. In this beautiful gift of this vision, I came to peace with the affirmation that they were in fact together and both okay. While I have not had such a vivid experience through Reiki since, it has brought me other tremendous gifts of healing through messages, visions, affirmations, and simply the feeling of balance and peace I feel afterward that I am eternally grateful for."

Jessica recalls how Reiki helped uncover anger that she didn't realize she even had. Her family was extremely traditional, but it never bothered her because it's how she grew up. Through her sessions, she began to realize she had deep resentment and subtle anger toward her parents. Reiki helped to draw out that resentment so she could see it for the first time. Subsequent sessions helped to heal and transmute these feelings so that she could fully appreciate her parents and understand where they were coming from and the culture that they grew up in.

A fellow Reiki master teacher, **Diana**, had to teach an upcoming segment on self-care at a class over the weekend. She practiced at home by teaching the self-care to her baby girl, who ended up falling asleep and took the longest morning nap ever. Diana hoped that she wouldn't have the same effect with her real students.

Cecilia was a forty-three-year-old doctor with young girls. Her oldest daughter, **Mia**, at eight years old had a lot of anxiety and very severe case of emetophobia, fear of throwing up. Cecilia was skeptical initially about Reiki, but was willing to try anything that might help. Before coming, she explained to her daughter that the session would be similar to a massage, but with a much lighter touch. Mia was nervous at first, but she felt safe and started to relax as the session began. She felt warmth through her body. As Mia put it, she was so relaxed she felt as if she were butter melting. She also felt intense heat at points in time. Her feet, according to her, were burning up as if they were a roast in an oven.

Mia had consistent regular sessions that helped her significantly break through her phobia. Soon after, Cecilia's youngest, **Tina**, also wanted to experience Reiki as well. Tina, at five years old, was extremely articulate. In her first session, she felt energy moving through her body and her fingers. In her words, she described the feeling as "unusual and not normal." Tina enjoyed Reiki very much. With her daughters enjoying Reiki so much, Cecilia decided to book some sessions and not long after went on to study Reiki herself.

Cecilia's grandmother had broken her hip and had been in the hospital where she developed pneumonia. Her health had deteriorated quickly and she was dying. However, as much as she had deteriorated, she was still hanging on. A relative of Cecilia's started sending distance Reiki to her grandmother. The relative also asked that everyone send recorded messages and calls to comfort the grandmother as well. And finally, two days later her grandmother passed. This experience allowed Cecilia's mother to open to Reiki as well because the experience was so profound and clearly related from her perspective. Cecilia's mother is now looking to learn Reiki as well.

At any given point in time, **Dean** and **Katy** would have at least three to five companion animals in their care for many years. They had started with two rescued shelter cats, Kiki and Felix, and cared for Katy's parents' two dogs often as well. Eventually, they added a neighborhood cat they named Piggy and another shelter pup to their menagerie. Dean and Katy were familiar with Reiki. It was most memorable when Piggy, who was around twelve, become very ill very quickly. She was diagnosed with severe renal failure. There was nothing the vet could do, so he sent them home to just comfort Piggy in her last remaining hours. As they recall, everything happened so fast, as the last hours were filled with so much confusion, uncertainty, and reluctance to accept what was actually happening. Their cousin sent distance Reiki and had them play healing mantra music, which calmed the chaos and eliminated the dread. Initially after getting back from the vet, Piggy was gasping and writhing about, but soon after Reiki began, she became very restful, which allowed them to offer more comfort to her as their alarm and sadness calmed. It was clear that Reiki comforted them all during an extremely difficult time.

how to meditate

"You have power over your mind—not outside events.
Realize this, and you will find strength."
—MARCUS AURELIUS

Meditation is key for Reiki practitioners. Anyone interested in learning Reiki would be well advised to cultivate a meditation practice. And even for those simply interested in receiving Reiki, meditation would be very helpful as well. If you are interested in further exploring Reiki and booking a session, you'll really get your money's worth if you've explored or at least just gotten familiar with your own inner workings and have a better understanding of your inner landscape. In this way, you are more open to sensing energy and shifts within yourself. There's no better time than the present to start

a meditation practice, and the good news is that it doesn't require much to get started.

Let's begin then, shall we?

Let's first define what the main goal is during meditation.

Ask yourself a few questions:

- ❀ **What outcome are we trying to achieve when we cultivate a meditation practice?**

- ❀ **Why do I want to meditate? For stress release? Less anxiety? Less reactivity?**

- ❀ **What outcome do I want for myself?**

A regular meditation practice brings a host of benefits like stress reduction, a strengthened immune system, increased gray matter in the brain (making you smarter, apparently), and a lengthening of your telomeres, which ultimately keeps you younger. These could be some of the reasons you'd want to start meditating. Or maybe you just want a little peace and quiet from the never-ending chatter in your mind. Meditation can help with that—not by shutting it off, but rather by teaching you how to hone your focus instead. When you meditate, that chatter becomes white noise in the background, kind of in the same way you can have the TV on in the background as you are totally immersed in something else, and you only tune back in when there's something of interest on the screen.

And beyond that, one of the biggest benefits is that meditation allows us to get to know ourselves better. You may think, "Oh, I know myself plenty." But do you really? Our unconscious mind is really skilled at hiding all kinds of old unresolved issues way below the baseline, the kind that only pop up at inopportune moments when a seemingly small incident triggers us. What if you could tune in to that bubbling up before a triggered meltdown? A regular meditation practice won't necessarily stop a full-on meltdown, but it could lessen its severity, and the moment of coming back to your senses will come sooner. The space between reaction and recovery and realization will be shorter. Maybe you'll have the reaction and then minutes later you realize that you overreacted and that it's not about the other person or what happened, it's really about you and your own issues. And when that occurs, wouldn't it be nice to identify what happened so that you can begin to work through it? Haven't you been carrying that issue around long enough? Awareness gives us the space to identify and do our inner work.

Meditation is about expanding awareness. It is about beginning to hone your awareness so that you can sense when something is rising to the surface, so that even if you aren't fully conscious of what's happening, you can allow yourself to follow that trail of breadcrumbs back to its source.

When we think about meditation in terms of the Reiki system, it's that we ultimately want to get to know ourselves better. When we have a regular meditation practice, we are expanding our awareness about ourselves and the world around us. We are getting curious about ourselves and about our reactions on the emotional and physical level. Maybe we begin to correlate the physical to the emotional and vice versa. Maybe we begin to notice that there is no randomness in the universe. When we begin to notice and realize that we are co-creators in our reality, we can tune in and see the patterns and make choices that support our destiny instead of being consigned to fate.

Through developing a meditation practice, we can tune in to subtle changes during a Reiki session: maybe noticing slight heat or cold, maybe noticing tingling or a slight feeling of constriction or opening. All of these are signs to tune in to the energy that's moving and shifting in our body and in our system. So that's the why, and hopefully we have some conscious and unconscious buy-in to meditate based on many of those reasons.

All that separates medication and meditation is one letter. Perhaps with a little more meditation, we can do with just a little less medication. With meditation, we seek to access our own inner wisdom—to know something for ourselves instead of being told. We seek to have our own experience of truth. Our truth. What may be true for one person may not be true for another, but ultimately when we all live our truth, therein lies freedom. Freedom to let go of "should" and freedom to be exactly who we are meant to be in this lifetime.

BUILDING A MEDITATION PRACTICE

When I work with my students and clients in starting a meditation practice, I like to set everyone up for success. And success means starting small. Baby steps are way more attainable when you are building a practice. Small incremental steps and consistency are the keys to creating a steady habit.

Just Start: Week 1

Find a comfortable place to sit. Maybe that's seated in a chair, letting go of any idea of sitting in a "perfect" meditation pose. You don't need to sit cross-legged on a meditation cushion on the floor to meditate unless that's comfortable for you. Sit where you are comfortable, but not too comfortable like when you sink into a cushy chair with no structure. You can even sit at the edge of your bed. (Hint: meditating as soon as your feet hit the ground in the morning is a lot easier than trying to meditate in the middle of the day!) However you are seated, see if you can sit with a mostly straight spine—maybe this takes some time to develop, and that's okay. Be okay with wherever you are in this process. This is also a metaphor for life—learning to be okay with whatever part of the journey you are at in life.

Once you've found a comfortable seat, sit upright, spine as straight as can be without straining, even, if necessary, seated back in a chair. Allow your hands to rest on your legs. Tune in to the weight of your body being supported, and just bring your attention to your breath. Watch as your breath moves in and as your breath moves out. With each breath in and each breath out, maybe add a mantra of sorts as you inhale. As you inhale, hear the word "let," and as you exhale, hear "go."

Continue for as long as you like, for a minimum of three minutes. As you breathe in "let "and breathe out "go," you are doing just that: letting go. Letting go through your breath. You are allowing yourself to be present with your own presence. And just this can be your meditation practice as you begin. Start with three minutes, and build incrementally, sitting a little longer every day until you find yourself sitting for eleven minutes or twenty minutes, and maybe even for up to half an hour at some point. But, really, three to five minutes is an excellent amount of time to sit and just get meditating already. Do this for a week or so and then move to the next level.

Keep Up: Week 2 and Onward

If you are ready to take it to the next level, you can start with the inhale on "let" and the exhale on "go" for a few minutes, and when you feel your body and your mind begin to settle, just allow the breath to be as it is. There is nothing to do here but just pay attention as breath moves in and breath moves out. Thoughts will come and go. Sensations, feelings, and emotions may pop up—just acknowledge them and come back to your breath each and every time you notice that you are no longer focused on breathing. Go easy on yourself when you notice your focus has drifted. This is normal. This is how you build the meditation "muscle." This is how you build awareness. So, gently bring yourself back to your breath. And that's it. Simple, yet oh-so-challenging. Again, start with just a few minutes at a time, but commit to a daily practice. Five minutes every day is doable, but the trick lies in the actual doing. So set yourself up for success—a great time to meditate is first thing in the morning. Wake up, sit up, and meditate. Get those five minutes in before the day starts, before your mind starts running down that never-ending to-do list.

Once you build a habit of taking time to sit in stillness and just watching breath, your awareness will begin to build. Slowly but surely, when we sit in stillness, stuff will start to rise up. Feelings and emotions that aren't so comfortable will bubble up. And we simply allow ourselves to be with it. Sit with the feelings and emotions, using breath to help you move through and simply be with what is. And by simply learning to be with what is, no matter how ugly or uncomfortable, we begin to create space for that energy to unwind. We are no longer in denial or avoidance. It is when we deny, avoid, and resist that these feelings get pushed down further, and the further and the harder you push them down, the stronger they will come up at some point, like pushing a volleyball deep under water and letting go.

During meditation, we are simply learning to be with what is. And by acknowledging what is, the energy around these feelings and emotions can begin to unwind. Through meditation, we want to develop the awareness to recognize the truth within ourselves.

Through meditation, we can maybe begin to realize there is more to life than just this physical body and experience. We can experience Reiki, the life-force energy all around us, the energy in our breath, in the trees, in the warmth of sunlight and the gentle breeze on our skin, in the flutter of a sparrow's wings, in the grains of sand, and in the vast ocean, the energy that connects everything in this universe.

When we begin to awaken to something greater than ourselves, something more than just this physical, gross level of matter, we open to spirit.

SOME MEDITATION FAQS

Meditation is so hard. I have a hard time just watching my breath; are there other types of meditation that I can try?

Yes, of course! There are so many different types and sources of meditation, everything from guided meditation apps with visualization to mantra meditation to staring at an object (otherwise known as tratakum meditation), and so much more. Experiment and see what works for you.

Why do people sit crossed-legged to meditate?

The traditional image associated with meditation is a person seated in a crossed leg position, because sitting in this way is unusual for most people. When we sit cross-legged, we are training our body and mind because we are seated differently than how we normally would. By beginning to anchor our body in this different way of sitting, we can then draw our focus inward. But if you can't sit cross-legged on the floor, no worries. What really matters is that your spine is straight, however you sit, whether crossed leg on the floor or in a chair.

During my meditation, there's a constant barrage of thoughts. What can I do to stop those thoughts and focus?

The good news is that if you feel overwhelmed by a million thoughts, that is how it's supposed to be! There's no stopping your mind. There will always be thoughts: that's what the brain does. It's designed to give input and commentary. When we practice meditation, we learn to choose what we focus on and how we focus. We allow the thoughts to be as they are, and we choose to focus on breath instead.

Meditation always makes me tired—why?

This comment often comes up often after my corporate group sessions. It's not the meditation that makes you tired. You were already tired and just didn't realize it. By taking the time to sit, we begin to notice things that we may have been oblivious to. With meditation, you can finally begin to listen to what your body needs. And if you are tired after meditation, that most likely means you need more rest!

Whenever I sit down to meditate, I often get fidgety, itchy, and twitchy. It's difficult not to move around. But why is it so important to sit still?

It's often been said that meditation is a clearing process. There's the analogy of: when you sit to meditate, think of yourself as a glass of muddy water. By sitting still, you are allowing the mud to separate from the water. We want that water to be clear. We want clarity. When we itch and move, we get stirred up and dirty the water, and then we need to start all over again.

COUNTING MEDITATION EXERCISE

This simple meditation is excellent for beginners. You simply choose a number to count to, like fifty or one hundred.

Sit comfortably in a chair or cross-legged on the ground. Close your eyes. Slow your breath down and begin counting on each inhale or each exhale—choose the count, and choose whether you are counting on the inhale or on the exhale, but not both. If you lose track of your count, simply begin again. Do not berate yourself: just begin again. This meditation helps to direct your focus and lets you be with breath. And maybe somewhere along the way, you will drift into an in-between neutral space while still tracking your count.

Once you've reached your number, you will have slowed the breath and relaxed a little more. End by taking a deep breath in and out, and just sitting in stillness for another minute or two to finish.

10

how to develop spirituality

"An unexamined life is not worth living."
—SOCRATES

Spirituality is what is related to spirit. Spirit is often defined as the vital principle held to give life to physical organisms, a supernatural essence, the immaterial part of a person. It is Reiki, life-force energy.

Spirituality is our connection to spirit, to the essence of who we are beyond the physical vehicle of our bodies and the material world. Beyond our conscious and logical minds and our will and our doing lies the flow of the universe. Developing our spirituality is a natural progression which comes when we begin to observe and open our awareness, when we may begin to encounter experiences that defy logic and reason. Spirituality is our connection to something greater than ourselves.

How do we develop our spirituality? How do we learn to trust that there is something greater than ourselves at work? How do we know that there is more to life than just our day-to-day existence?

If we want to think about how to develop our spirituality in the context of Reiki, we can go right back to the one thing that Master Usui taught all his students, the Reiki precepts: "Just for today, don't worry." "Just for today, don't anger." When we begin with those lines, Master Usui helps us get out of day-to-day patterns of worry and reactiveness. And we don't have to think of it as a huge commitment . . . *just for today* is a great place to start. When we begin to break little reactive patterns of worry and anger, we create a little space for ourselves, space for awareness. By creating space and expanding awareness, we can begin to see the hand of the universe in all things. Sound a little much for you? No problem, just start to pay attention to your life and you might begin to notice the universe speaking to you in subtle and often not-so-subtle ways.

A few years ago, I took a big leap in signing a commercial lease for my healing space. The short version of how this story begins is that all kinds of doors opened for me so that I could get the lease—this was the universe working for me. But where I started out nervous and excited, once I had the space, it brought up a lot of unconscious fear and resistance. In the course of getting the space ready, I kept having air-conditioning issues. I went through three different air conditioners over the course of a few months—the first one was the wrong size, the second one didn't work well. It was midsummer, and I couldn't really use the space and have class and clients without proper air-conditioning. I finally decided that I needed to spend the extra money and get the proper AC, which came with a more expensive installation.

On the day of the installation, I noticed that I was strangely nervous. I realized that once the AC was installed properly, I would have no more excuses—I had to step up and take my space and use it. (And let me assure you, I definitely did not have the budget to be paying rent and not use it—see how strong resistance can be?) That afternoon, the guys who were going to do the work came and installed the AC, and when they turned it on, it wouldn't start. I started laughing. The workers were perplexed and exclaimed that in all their twenty-plus years, this had never happened. I knew the reason was me and my energy, so instead of crying, I kept laughing—because I *knew*. They spent a few more minutes trying to tweak it and it finally started. The AC began working, but loudly, as if something was rattling inside. Needless to say, I still had a lot of resistance to work through.

When I finally worked it out with the manufacturer and got someone to come service my brand new unit, another several weeks had gone by. By now, I was working in my space, but with a loud AC that sounded like a propeller plane about to take off—not the most conducive sound for my healing sessions and workshops, but, luckily, most clients didn't mind. The manufacturer had estimated that my AC unit would be back in a week or so, but that dragged on for weeks, by which point the weather had cooled. It was another several weeks later, when they finally brought the unit back—the repair man chuckling the whole time—that we learned it had been delayed waiting for a part that we thought was missing, but it was just stuck inside the unit the whole time. Yes, that was me—me as the AC: I had everything I needed, but I was just stuck inside the entire time.

The universe is always communicating to us. Spirituality is developing the space and awareness to listen and hear.

The rest of the precepts are other ways of interacting with the universe. "Please accept everything and give thanks" means that we are not in control, we are not the ones who are doing the doing.

Give it up—let go and let the universe in. Surrender and trust is what this precept says. This is the work that is the hardest. We can begin with gratitude as a practice. Begin by being grateful every day. Don't just say it, don't just give it lip service. It has to be true. Find something that you are truly grateful for, and tapping in to that will change every single molecule in your being.

"Strive to embody the teachings in your actions. Be kind to others." Bring these teachings, these principles, into your everyday actions. Don't worry, don't get angry, accept all, be grateful, and be kind. That's it. Simple.

Take the time for yourself to observe and notice. Pay attention to the things that are drawing your attention. Ask yourself why. Not everything has to be something—don't make yourself crazy that way, don't overanalyze your life and not live it. Just be mindful. Notice the things that speak to you. Question why you are feeling what you are feeling. See if you can move through each layer. Get quiet and tune in to the whisperings of the universe. The universe is always communicating to us; are you listening?

Meditation is key to learning how to listen, but it's not the only way. You can listen to nature or listen to your body as you lie down to sleep. Simply intend to listen. Practice a little bit every day. Let the universe know that you are ready to listen. Build some time into the day, so that you are not always rushing. Give yourself space, even if it means getting up ten minutes earlier in the morning so that you have a few extra minutes. When we are rushing and busy, it's harder to hear.

You don't need a lot of time to slow down and listen. It's about tuning in to the right frequency and what you intend to listen to. I have a five-minute walk to the subway. I walk along a side street in my neighborhood that has some lovely trees. The first three trees are linden trees in big planters. Their trunks are straight and their leaves are extremely symmetrical in shape, like an elongated heart. The leaves are full and green this season. When I turn the corner, there are three more trees of the same kind. Extremely straight and smooth dark trunks, and for the first few years, they too have bloomed full and green. Year after year, day after day, I feel blessed by all the trees as I walk by. And in return, I send blessings back. This summer, they have areas where the leaves are yellowed and branches are dying out. When I first noticed this, I felt dismayed and sad. And as I felt this, it was as if the trees spoke to me—don't be sad, this is the cycle of life, some parts in bloom and healthy and full and other parts slowly declining. And as I continue my walk down the block, I pass some giant ginkgo trees. They are solid and tall and big with leaves that look like fans. They have been around for some time and it's as if they nod solemnly in their wisdom to back up what the other trees say—to remind me that this is all a continuous cycle—infinity, life, death, rebirth.

Now, all of this communication didn't just happen overnight. I've been developing a relationship with these trees. They came to my attention when I noticed one day how pretty and straight they were. A few days later, one branch was hanging low, filled with a bounty of leaves that touched my head as I walked beneath. I felt blessed. And so we began our communication. First, I began to notice them: their shape, their leaves, their color. And after more time passed, I began to notice even more about them. As we begin to take time to explore by observing, communication happens. We begin to tune in. Waves of understanding come and we get attuned to the frequency of the trees, or whatever it is you are focused on. That saying—"Where your attention goes, energy flows"—reminds us that what we choose to focus on is what we get attuned to the frequency of. When we think about waves in terms of energy, it's the properties of waves that allow information to be communicated. Waves of energy are encoded with information.

Practicing dreamwork is an excellent way to learn to listen. The unconscious mind speaks in metaphors, in stories through dreams. Perhaps this is an exercise that resonates with you: before going to bed, just set an intention of sorts—let your unconscious mind and your spirit know that you are open to listening, that you are ready to receive. Go to sleep. Now, when you first wake up, don't move. Lie still and see if you can recall parts of your dream. Just slowly and gently let yourself flow into any images or stories that you recall. Once you've firmly remembered, get up and write it down. More images and details may come flooding through as you write. Give your dream a title related to its theme that captures the feeling. And if you can't remember your dreams just yet, keep practicing with your intention before bed to be open to listening and remembering. Before you know it, you'll start to remember little bits and pieces and then full-on dreams.

People often seek Reiki to help with physical pain. A common way of thinking about physical pain in energetic terms is that your body is communicating with you. When you open up and begin to develop spiritually, it just means that you are willing to look at things differently and begin to question and listen.

Louise Hay of holistic healing publishing wrote the book *Heal Your Body* (Hay House, 1984) in which she discusses how pain in certain parts of the body is related to specific emotional issues. These are very general suggestions for inquiry. Nothing is ever the be-all, end-all. Get advice and help from your teachers and coaches and energy healers, but ultimately be your own guru and feel what resonates for you. Perhaps stop and listen to your body for a little bit before automatically reaching for the aspirin. Take a moment or two to sit with your discomfort. Breathe and listen to what your body wants you to know.

DREAMWORK EXERCISE

You could also use this dreamwork exercise to specifically work with pain in your body or to just ask your body what it needs you to know. Before going to bed, as you lie down, just let your body know that you are ready to listen to what the pain is trying to communicate— sure, it could just be something as simple as your body needing more rest, but aches and pains are usually attached to something deeper, if we want to explore further.

As you lie in bed, state something simple to yourself, such as, "I'm ready to listen to what my body and my unconscious mind are trying to tell me." And upon waking, lie very still and begin to recall your dream. And then write your dream down. Give thanks to your unconscious mind and body for whatever information you've received, even if the dream makes no sense yet. We are just starting to open up this channel of communication. And if you can't seem to recall your dreams right away, keep it up and the intention of wanting to remember your dreams will begin to come to fruition.

So choose your own level of exploration, but by simply acknowledging the pain in your body and by creating space through gentle inquiry, that could be all it takes to heal. By doing so, we open up another channel of communication and another channel of listening to the universe.

11

the illusion of good and bad energy

"Things are as they are. Looking out into the universe at night, we make no comparisons between right and wrong stars, nor between well and badly arranged constellations."
—ALAN WATTS

People often talk about good energy and bad energy. Reiki is life-force energy. It's the all-encompassing energy of oneness. Labeling things as good energy and bad energy extends this feeling of duality, which is actually an illusion. It is all manifestations of life-force energy. The trees let me know that there is nothing to be sad about as part of a tree dies, because all of this is a never-ending cycle of the flow of creation. When we label experiences as good and bad, we take away their truth. We take away from the learning and the wisdom that comes from going through tough and challenging life events and experiences. It is when we move through the "bad" that we experience growth. Without resistance and tension, we cannot grow. Brilliant crystals are created through great pressure and fire deep within the earth.

When clients come in feeling like they need more good energy, I gently remind them it's all just energy. It's just about balance. Life is a flow. We need pressure and tension to grow and force ourselves out of our comfort zone. There is no growth in comfort.

It's definitely challenging to think about energy as simply energy—not good energy, not bad energy, simply the energy that is at play in the moment. It's easy to label something as good or bad, but it may not be conducive to energy flow. We tend to want to hold on to ideals of good and not let go, either, of bad experiences. Perhaps we can start to think of things as being in balance or out of balance, being in alignment or out of alignment, instead of as good and bad.

When it comes to our own energy or others' energy around us, it's important to remember to keep judgment in check. Clients come in asking to clear out other people's bad energy that they feel that they have taken on. I want clients and everyone I encounter to feel empowered, to know that it is always their work to do, to keep clear, to strengthen their energy. Reiki brings energy into balance, strengthening the energetic field. When you are standing strong, you don't take on anyone's "bad" energy or anyone's anything. You are strong in your truth.

Remember that story about my little boy cat who was reflecting the stuck energy of myself and my partner and our relationship at the time? Well, the universe continued to send messages of stuck energy, culminating in the bathroom sink getting fully clogged. No problem, I figured—quick call to the super to snake the drain. The building maintenance guys came to snake the clog, and somehow the snake broke in the pipe. That stuck energy was potent. What should have been a quick fix turned into a bit of an ordeal over a few days. They took the sink apart to access the pipe, but the broken snake was not that easy to find. They ended up breaking through our bedroom wall to see if they could find the snake further along the pipe, still to no avail. Finally, they ended up finding the broken snake in the pipe after going through the downstairs neighbor's ceiling. We had to have several literal "breakthroughs" before we could move that stuck energy. After this, there was a palpable shift and our communication opened up.

Now, you could look at that story and chalk it up to bad luck or bad energy, or you could see the magic of the vibrational world at play. I chose to see the practical magic of the universe at play. And, at the time, it definitely didn't feel like play. But wouldn't life be different if we could view it through the lens of magic and play?

We are only here in this physical body for a short time. It is a limited edition and one of a kind. No time like the present to make the most of it. Bringing the Reiki system into your life can help jump-start tuning into your intuition and truth. It can guide you on to your path, your dharma—what you are meant to do and share with the world in this lifetime. Bringing to the world your magic because no one does it the way you do—that's your truth. Thank so much for joining us on this little Reiki primer. I trust that you received what you needed. I hope that it opens up your mind just by reading about it. I know it will open up your world when you experience it either through a session or by jumping in to learn the Reiki system for yourself. The Reiki system in its simplicity and ease of use will give you perspective, and freedom to be your authentic self. It will open you up to your multisensory human being. A certain commercial reappropriated tagline comes to mind: Essentially, Reiki gives you wings.

No time like the present to step fully into your radiant presence and experience the magic all around you.

ACKNOWLEDGMENTS

I wanted to thank Sterling Publishing for allowing me to share this little book in the big world. Thank you especially to Kate Zimmermann, for her intuition and the amazing opportunity to birth a book into being, as well as for her patient guidance and assistance. In deep gratitude to my teachers Margaret Ann Case, Joanna Crespo, Gary Strauss, and Guru Dharam Khalsa for all the wisdom and healing they so graciously shared and continue to share. Special thanks to my dear friend Julie Kim McMahon, who knew I had a book in me even when I didn't. Thank you so much to all who shared their healing stories with me. Thank you to my family and friends, for cheering me on throughout this writing process and beyond. Thank you, Francis Catania, for your most delicious pasta creations and for your love and support.

ENDNOTES

Chapter 1: Vibrational Universe

PAGE 2. "The fact is that what we 'know,' in terms of actual matter only accounts for about 4 percent of what makes up our universe; the rest of that 96 percent is unknown and unseen." Space.com: https://www.space.com/11642-dark-matter-dark-energy-4-percent-universe-panek.html.

PAGE 3. "Its purpose? To test particle physics and other unsolved questions, as well as to find other dimensions." CERN: https://home.cern/about/physics/extra-dimensions-gravitons-and-tiny-black-holes]

PAGE 3. "The science that matches this concept can be found in physics' superstring theory, which states that there are ten dimensions versus the standard three and the fourth dimension of time." PBS: http://www.pbs.org/wgbh/nova/blogs/physics/2014/04/how-many-dimensions-does-the-universe-really-have.

PAGE 3: "And then there's the concept of ancestral karma, which is now actually proven through the study of epigenetics: trauma and depression in families can actually be passed down through the outer sheath of DNA." Big Think: https://bigthink.com/philip-perry/the-bad-news-trauma-can-be-inherited-the-good-news-so-can-resilience.

PAGE 4: "According to Lorenz's Chaos Theory and the butterfly effect, the minuscule flapping of a butterfly's wings in one part of the world has the potential to create huge weather systems in another." *MIT Technology Review:* https://www.technologyreview.com/s/422809/when-the-butterfly-effect-took-flight.

PAGE 5: "'Humans are a fractal image of society, cells are a fractal image of the human. In fact, cells are a fractal image of society as well. The fractal nature of evolution is further implied by the reiterated, self-same patterns observed in each of the three cycles of evolution.'" Bruce Lipton: https://www.brucelipton.com/resource/article/fractal-evolution.

Chapter 6: Different Levels of Reiki

PAGE 55. "'Quantum entanglement is another term for the principle we want to understand in this post, quantum nonlocality, by which tiny objects initially interact, then move any distance apart and still impact one another.'" Deepak Chopra: https://www.huffingtonpost.com/deepak-chopra/how-to-see-the-whole-univ_b_9515722.html.

Chapter 9: How to Meditate

PAGE 84. "A regular meditation practice brings a host of benefits like stress reduction, a strengthened immune system, increased gray matter in the brain (making you smarter, apparently), and a lengthening of your telomeres, which ultimately keeps you younger." Dr. Paula Watkins: https://www.mindbodygreen.com/0-18628/how-meditation-lengthens-telomeres-improves-overall-brain-power.html.

Chapter 10: How to Develop Spirituality

PAGE 95. "Spirit is often defined as the vital principle held to give life to physical organisms, a supernatural essence, the immaterial part of a person." Merriam Webster: https://www.merriam-webster.com/dictionary/spirit.

BIBLIOGRAPHY

Interested in reading more about Reiki and diving into the world of vibrational energy?

Here are some further reading resources:

Dale, Cyndi. *The Subtle Body: An Encyclopedia of Your Energetic Anatomy.* Colorado: Sounds True, Inc., 2009.

Doi, Hiroshi. *A Modern Reiki Method for Healing.* Missouri: Vision Publications, 2014.

Gerber, Richard. *Vibrational Medicine: The #1 Handbook of Subtle-Energy Therapies.* Vermont: Bear & Company, 2001.

Judith, Anodea. *Eastern Body Western Mind (Revised): Psychology and the Chakra System as a Path to the Self.* New York: Celestial Arts–Crown Publishing Group–Random House, Inc., 2004.

Lipton, Bruce. *The Biology of Belief: Unleashing the Power of Consciousness, Matter & Miracles.* Carlsbad: Hay House, Inc., 2016.

McTaggart, Lynne. *The Field: The Quest for the Secret Force of the Universe.* New York: Harper-Collins Publishers, 2008.

Pert, Candace. *Molecules of Emotion: The Science Behind Mind–Body Medicine.* New York: Scribner, 2003.

Singer, Michael. *The Untethered Soul: The Journey Beyond Yourself.* Oakland: New Harbinger, 2007.

Stiene, Bronwen and Frans. *The Reiki Sourcebook.* New York: O Books, 2003.

INDEX

A

Ancestral karma, 3
Anger, and Reiki treatment, 78–79
Animals, Reiki for, 45–47
Attunements, 14–15
Aurelius, Marcus, 83
"Authentic Reiki." See Radiance Technique

B

"Bad" energy, 105–107
"Biofield therapy," 10–11
Biology of Belief, The, 5
Buddhism, 23
Butterfly effect, 4

C

Campbell, Joseph, 23
Cats, and Reiki treatment
  crystals, 47
  death of, 77–78
  with leaky eye, 71–72
  seeking permission from, 45
  shelter, 80–81
Channel, definition of, 10
Chaos Theory, 4
Chinese medicine
  dan tien, 21
  meridians, 16
  and Reiki, 2
Chopra, Deepak, 54–55
Connect Heaven to Earth exercise, 29
Connect to Earth exercise, 28
Connect to Heaven exercise, 28
Counting meditation exercise, 92–93
Creating space (in life), 31, 64–66
Crystal Reiki, 39

D

Dahl, Roald, vi
Dan tien, 21
Dark energy, 2
Dark matter, 2
Depression, and ancestral karma, 3
Dharma, 108
Disease, and Reiki, 11–12
Donne, John, 48
Dreamwork, practicing, 101, 101–103

E

Earth, connecting to, 28, 29
Eco, Umberto, 37
Einstein, Albert, 31
Emetophobia, and Reiki treatment, 77
Empowered recipient, 19–20
Energy, 105–108
Evolution, fractal, 31
Exercises
  basic, ix–x
  counting meditation, 92–93
  dreamwork, 102–103
  ground and elevate, 27–29
  receive and flow, 48–49
  strengthening your power, 20–21
  tuning in, 35
  universal connection, 67
  vibrational universe, 6–7

F

Fibroids, using Reiki to treat, 70–71
Fractal cosmology, 5

G

Gendai Reiki, 38
"Good energy," 105–107
Grade school, using Reiki to prepare for, 70

Ground and elevate exercise, 27–29

H

Hay, Louise, 102
Hayashi, Chujiro, 26–27
Heal Your Body, 102
Healing, moments of, 69–81
Heaven, connecting to, 28
Holy Fire Reiki, 39

I

Indian yogic tradition, and "nadis," 16
Ishikuro, Iris, 38

J

Jikiden Reiki, 38
Jung, Carl, 33

K

Kabbalah, and Reiki, 2, 3
Karma, ancestral, 3
Karuna Reiki, 39
Komyo Reiki, 38
Kundalini Reiki, 39

L

Lao Tzu, 59
Levels of Reiki, 14–15, 51–54
Life Energy Institute, 27
Lipton, Dr. Bruce, 5, 31
Loneliness, using Reiki to deal with, 77
Lorenz's Chaos Theory, 4
Loss of father, using Reiki to deal with, 76

M

Marriage breakup, using Reiki to deal with, 74
Master level of Reiki, 53–54
Meditation
  experience, guided, 6–7
  FAQs, 90–92
  first experience with, 75–76
  importance to Reiki practitioners, 83

Meditation (*Continued*)
  practice, 83–87
  practice, building a, 87–90
Meridians, 16
Migraines, using Reiki to
    deal with, 74–75
Milner, Kathleen, 39
Mount Kurama, 24
Mount Sinai Beth Israel
    Hospital, 11
Mudras, 4–5

N

Nadis, 16
Name of the Rose, The, 37

P

Polarity therapy, 5
Post-operative patients, and
    Reiki, 11
Practitioner, Reiki
  and attunements, 14–15
  author's first experience
      with a, viii–ix
  caring for himself/herself,
      12–13
  and channel, 10
  and distance healing,
      54–57
  early, 24–27
  finding a, 59–60
  and levels, 51–54
  and Master Usui's system,
      40–41
  and meditation, 83–93
  and moments of healing,
      69–81
  and permission from
      recipients, 43
  and polarity therapy, 5
  and sessions, 16–19
  and session, during a,
      61–64
  and session, preparing
      for, 61
  what they do, 9

Q

Qi Gong, 40–41
Quantum physics
  and distance healing,
      54–55
  and vibrational universe, 4

R

Radiance Technique, 39
Raku Kei Reiki, 38–39
Rand, William Lee, 39
Ray, Dr. Barbara, 39
"Real Reiki." *See* Radiance
    Technique
Receive and flow exercise,
    48–49
Reiki
  for animals, 45–47
  author's first experience
      with, viii–ix
  and creating space in your
      life, 31, 64–66
  and disease, 11–12
  effects and benefits, 32
  and empowered recipient,
      19–20
  as energy work, 10–11
  funding for studying, 11
  ground and elevate
      exercise, 27–29
  as hands-on healing
      modality, vi, x–xi, 12
  levels and attunements,
      14–15, 51–54
  origin and history, 23–27
  origin of word, 9
  permission to receive,
      42–44
  and personal and spiritual
      growth, 12
  power exercise,
      strengthening, 20–21
  receive and flow exercise,
      48–49
  session, 16–19, 61–64

sharing, 13, 44
  and synchronicity, 32–35
  system of natural healing,
      23
  tuning in exercise, 35
  types of, 37–42
  what system is, 9
  what term means, ix
Robertson, Arthur, 38
Rumi, 9

S

Seagull, and Reiki, 45–46
Seated, cross-legged
    meditation, 87–88, 91
Seichem, 39
Shamanic Reiki, 39
Sharing Reiki, 13, 44
Shintoism, 23–24
Sinus issues, using Reiki to
    deal with, 73–75
Socrates, 95
Space (in life), creating, 31,
    64–66
Spirituality, developing,
    95–103
Stone, Dr. Randolph, 5
Strauss, Gary, 27
Synchronicity, and Reiki,
    32–35

T

Takata, Hawayo
  and development of Reiki,
      26–27
  and initiation of twenty-
      two Reiki masters,
      37–38
  and Radiance Technique,
      39
Tera Mai system, 39
Tesla, Nikola, 1
Trauma, and ancestral
    karma, 3
Tuning in exercise, 35
Tyson, Neil DeGrasse, 51

U

Universal connection exercise, 66, 67
Universal healing energy, 10
Universal Position, 67
Universe, and energy, 1–7
Usui, Mikao, ix, 23–26
Usui Reiki Ryoho, 25, 38
Usui/Tibetan Reiki, 39

V

Vibrational universe
  balancing out elements of nature, 4, 5
  dark energy, 2
  dark matter, 2
  and energy, 1–6
  exercise, 6
  and fractal cosmology, 5
  and Kabbalah, 3
  Lorenz's Chaos Theory, 4
  polarity therapy, 5
  and quantum physics, 4
  and science, 2

W

Watts, Alan, 105

X

Zeigler, Patrick, 39

ABOUT THE AUTHOR

Valerie Oula is the founder of Modern Ritual NYC, a holistic lifestyle offering for mind, body, and soul. She is a KRI-certified Kundalini Yoga Instructor and has been sharing Reiki since 2007. She shares her passion for vibrational medicine through healing sessions, classes, workshops, events, and trainings.

Valerie creates an energetic haven for students and clients to unwind, process, and heal through kundalini yoga, Reiki, and other healing modalities. Having been blessed with the spiritual name Saranjeet Kaur (*Saran* means sanctuary, *Jeet* means victory, *Kaur* is the Lioness of God), Valerie strives to create sacred space for all to overcome obstacles and walk the path of victory.

While walking the path of victory, Valerie is almost always in search of delicious vegan eats and is slightly obsessed with massive pink halite crystal clusters. She lives in New York City with her life partner and their two beautiful cats, BooBoo and Theo.

Reach out via Instagram @valerieoula @modernritualnyc and visit www.modernritualnyc.com to learn more.